MACMILLAN MAS[TER...]

GENERAL EDITOR: JAMES GIBSON

Published

JANE AUSTEN	*Emma* Norman Page
	Sense and Sensibility Judy Simons
	Persuasion Judy Simons
	Pride and Prejudice Raymond Wilson
	Mansfield Park Richard Wirdnam
SAMUEL BECKETT	*Waiting for Godot* Jennifer Birkett
WILLIAM BLAKE	*Songs of Innocence* and *Songs of Experience* Alan Tomlinson
ROBERT BOLT	*A Man for all Seasons* Leonard Smith
EMILY BRONTË	*Wuthering Heights* Hilda D. Spear
GEOFFREY CHAUCER	*The Miller's Tale* Michael Alexander
	The Pardoner's Tale Geoffrey Lester
	The Wife of Bath's Tale Nicholas Marsh
	The Knight's Tale Anne Samson
	The Prologue to the Canterbury Tales Nigel Thomas and Richard Swan
JOSEPH CONRAD	*The Secret Agent* Andrew Mayne
CHARLES DICKENS	*Bleak House* Dennis Butts
	Great Expectations Dennis Butts
	Hard Times Norman Page
GEORGE ELIOT	*Middlemarch* Graham Handley
	Silas Marner Graham Handley
	The Mill on the Floss Helen Wheeler
HENRY FIELDING	*Joseph Andrews* Trevor Johnson
E. M. FORSTER	*Howards End* Ian Milligan
	A Passage to India Hilda D. Spear
WILLIAM GOLDING	*The Spire* Rosemary Sumner
	Lord of the Flies Raymond Wilson
OLIVER GOLDSMITH	*She Stoops to Conquer* Paul Ranger
THOMAS HARDY	*The Mayor of Casterbridge* Ray Evans
	Tess of the d'Urbervilles James Gibson
	Far from the Madding Crowd Colin Temblett-Wood
JOHN KEATS	*Selected Poems* John Garrett
PHILIP LARKIN	*The Whitsun Weddings* and *The Less Deceived* Andrew Swarbrick
D. H. LAWRENCE	*Sons and Lovers* R. P. Draper
HARPER LEE	*To Kill a Mockingbird* Jean Armstrong
GERARD MANLEY HOPKINS	*Selected Poems* R. J. C. Watt
CHRISTOPHER MARLOWE	*Doctor Faustus* David A. Male
VIRGINIA WOOLF	*To the Lighthouse* John Mepham
THE METAPHYSICAL POETS	Joan van Emden

MACMILLAN MASTER GUIDES

THOMAS MIDDLETON and WILLIAM ROWLEY	*The Changeling* Tony Bromham
ARTHUR MILLER	*The Crucible* Leonard Smith *Death of a Salesman* Peter Spalding
GEORGE ORWELL	*Animal Farm* Jean Armstrong
WILLIAM SHAKESPEARE	*Richard II* Charles Barber *Hamlet* Jean Brooks *King Lear* Francis Casey *Henry V* Peter Davison *The Winter's Tale* Diana Devlin *Julius Caesar* David Elloway *Macbeth* David Elloway *Measure for Measure* Mark Lilly *Henry IV Part I* Helen Morris *Romeo and Juliet* Helen Morris *The Tempest* Kenneth Pickering *A Midsummer Night's Dream* Kenneth Pickering *Coriolanus* Gordon Williams *Antony and Cleopatra* Martin Wine
GEORGE BERNARD SHAW	*St Joan* Leonée Ormond
RICHARD SHERIDAN	*The School for Scandal* Paul Ranger *The Rivals* Jeremy Rowe
ALFRED TENNYSON	*In Memoriam* Richard Gill
ANTHONY TROLLOPE	*Barchester Towers* Ken Newton
JOHN WEBSTER	*The White Devil* and *The Duchess of Malfi* David A. Male

Forthcoming

CHARLOTTE BRONTË	*Jane Eyre* Robert Miles
JOHN BUNYAN	*The Pilgrim's Progress* Beatrice Batson
T. S. ELIOT	*Murder in the Cathedral* Paul Lapworth *Selected Poems* Andrew Swarbrick
BEN JONSON	*Volpone* Michael Stout
RUDYARD KIPLING	*Kim* Leonée Ormond
JOHN MILTON	*Comus* Tom Healy
WILLIAM SHAKESPEARE	*Othello* Tony Bromham *As You Like It* Kiernan Ryan
VIRGINIA WOOLF	*Mrs Dalloway* Julian Pattison
W. B. YEATS	*Selected Poems* Stan Smith

MACMILLAN MASTER GUIDES

MRS DALLOWAY

BY VIRGINIA WOOLF

JULIAN PATTISON

© Julian Pattison 1987

All rights reserved. No reproduction, copy or transmission of this publication may be made without written permission.

No paragraph of this publication may be reproduced, copied or transmitted save with written permission or in accordance with the provisions of the Copyright Act 1956 (as amended) or under the terms of any licence permitting limited copying issued by the Copyright Licensing Agency, 33–4 Alfred Place, London WC1E 7PP.

Any person who does any unauthorised act in relation to this publication may be liable to criminal prosecution and civil claims for damages.

First edition 1987

Published by
MACMILLAN EDUCATION LTD
Houndmills, Basingstoke, Hampshire RG21 2XS
and London
Companies and representatives
throughout the world

Typeset in Great Britain by
TEC SET, Wallington, Surrey

Printed in Hong Kong

British Library Cataloguing in Publication Data
Pattison, Julian
Mrs Dalloway: by Virginia Woolf.—
(Macmillan master guides).
1. Woolf, Virginia. Mrs Dalloway
I. Title II. Woolf, Virginia. Mrs Dalloway
823'.912   PR6045.O7M5
ISBN 0–333–43700–4 Pbk
ISBN 0–333–43701–2 Pbk export

CONTENTS

General editor's preface   vii

Acknowledgements   viii

1	**Virginia Woolf: life and background**			1
2	**Summaries and critical commentary**	2.1	Introduction	10
		2.2–12	Summaries and commentaries	13
3	**Themes and issues**	3.1	The life and death of the soul	47
		3.2	Identity and loneliness	49
		3.3	Madness	51
		3.4	*Mrs Dalloway* as a social satire	52
		3.5	London	54
4	**Techniques**	4.1	Narrative method	59
		4.2	Methods of characterization	63
		4.3	Imagery	66
5	**Specimen passage and commentary**	5.1	Specimen passage	69
		5.2	Commentary	70
6	**Critical appraisals**	6.1	Contemporary criticism	73
		6.2	More modern criticism	76

Revision questions   79

Further reading   81

GENERAL EDITOR'S PREFACE

The aim of the Macmillan Master Guides is to help you to appreciate the book you are studying by providing information about it and by suggesting ways of reading and thinking about it which will lead to a fuller understanding. The section on the writer's life and background has been designed to illustrate those aspects of the writer's life which have influenced the work, and to place it in its personal and literary context. The summaries and critical commentary are of special importance in that each brief summary of the action is followed by an examination of the significant critical points. The space which might have been given to repetitive explanatory notes has been devoted to a detailed analysis of the kind of passage which might confront you in an examination. Literary criticism is concerned with both the broader aspects of the work being studied and with its detail. The ideas which meet us in reading a great work of literature, and their relevance to us today, are an essential part of our study, and our Guides look at the thought of their subject in some detail. But just as essential is the craft with which the writer has constructed his work of art, and this may be considered under several technical headings – characterisation, language, style and stagecraft, for example.

The authors of these Guides are all teachers and writers of wide experience, and they have chosen to write about books they admire and know well in the belief that they can communicate their admiration to you. But you yourself must read and know intimately the book you are studying. No one can do that for you. You should see this book as a lamp-post. Use it to shed light, not to lean against. If you know your text and know what it is saying about life, and how it says it, then you will enjoy it, and there is no better way of passing an examination in literature.

JAMES GIBSON

ACKNOWLEDGEMENTS

The author and publishers wish to thank the following who has kindly given permission for the use of copyright material: The Hogarth Press Ltd and the Estate of Virginia Woolf for extracts from *Mrs Dalloway* by Virginia Woolf.

Every effort has been made to trace all the copyright holders but if any have been inadvertently overlooked the publishers will be pleased to make the necessary arrangement at the first opportunity.

Cover illustration: *The Black Hat* by Francis Campbell Boileau Cadell, courtesy of the City of Edinburgh Museums and Art Galleries.

1 VIRGINIA WOOLF: LIFE AND BACKGROUND

Virginia Stephen was born on 25 January, 1882 at 22 Hyde Park Gate, London, within easy reach of the part of London which forms the setting for *Mrs. Dalloway*. She was the third child (the others were Vanessa, Thoby and Adrian) of Sir Leslie Stephen's marriage to Julia Duckworth (née Pattle) in 1878. Both parents had been married before, so the family was both large and diverse. From the Duckworth side came three children: George, Stella and Gerald. From the Stephen side came Laura who, like Virginia, inherited the family madness.

The family was dominated by Virginia's parents. Both came from upper-middle-class families who had in their time known some of the most eminent of Victorian writers, artists and thinkers. Sir Leslie's father had been a civil servant and had also been devoted to a branch of benevolent Christianity known as the Clapham sect. His son followed in this, taking Holy Orders in 1859 in order to be able to take up a Fellowship at Trinity Hall, Cambridge, but then resigning when it became obvious that he could no longer subscribe to Christian doctrine. From then on he devoted himself to writing literary biography, philosophy and literary criticism. Today he is chiefly remembered as the editor of the gigantic *Dictionary of National Biography*. His influence on Virginia was considerable, for from early childhood she was surrounded with books and talk about books. However, despite her obvious literary interests and intellectual talents, she was largely self-taught because Cambridge, where her father and her brothers had been educated, was still largely closed to women. Her education, gleaned haphazardly from her parents, was sound but unbalanced.

In later life Virginia viewed her upbringing as having had two sides. Whilst the intellectual side of her came from Sir Leslie, the artistic and creative side of her life was, she felt, inherited from the Pattles, who had mixed with the cream of the Victorian creative élite such as the pre-Raphaelite artists Holman Hunt and Edward Burne-Jones and the writers Alfred Tennyson and William Makepeace Thackeray. Vanessa gave herself over entirely to this side of the family by becoming a painter of considerable talent; Virginia on the other hand attempted to combine both elements of her inheritance by becoming both a novelist and a critic.

Virginia's adolescence was blighted by a number of traumatic events. Her mother Julia died in 1895, and as a direct consequence of this Virginia succumbed for the first time to the madness which was to shadow her throughout her life and which she tries to portray through the character of Septimus Smith in *Mrs Dalloway*. Shortly after the death of her mother came another: that of her half-sister Stella; and then in 1904 and 1906 the deaths of Sir Leslie and her brother Thoby. The remaining children found themselves very much on their own. In an effort to escape from the unpleasant associations of 22 Hyde Park Gate they moved and set up house together at 46 Gordon Square, Bloomsbury. It was here that the famous Bloomsbury group began to form. At first, it consisted almost entirely of Adrian and Thoby's friends from Cambridge. However, as the group expanded many now famous artists and thinkers became involved, including John Maynard Keynes, the economist; Lytton Strachey, the eccentric author of *Eminent Victorians*; and Clive Bell, the painter, who became Vanessa's husband in 1907. As the years went past, other figures such as the novelist E. M. Forster and the poet T. S. Eliot became associated with Bloomsbury. At the centre of the group's thought was a commitment to innovation and experimentalism and a determination to shake off the influence of the Victorians. G. E. Moore, the Cambridge philosopher who had influenced many of them, contributed the theory of an 'intellectual aristocracy' which espoused the idea of a civilization based on mental prowess and creativity and therefore showed contempt both for the vulgarity of the middle classes and for the limitations of the uncivilized ruling classes. Even though the members of the Bloomsbury group were in a way a product of the establishment which they sought to criticize, they felt that they stood outside the values of a ruling class – that of the Dalloways – which devoted itself to 'civilizing' and governing an empire. Indeed, during the First World War their stance was made obvious (and much resented) when a number of them declared that they were conscientious objectors.

Initially the group offered Virginia the education that she felt she had missed through not going to university. And its abandonment of Victorian values, both moral and artistic, was crucial to her development as a writer. However, she did not merely become a mouthpiece for the group: instead, she viewed it from a distance in her works. For example, in *Mrs Dalloway* both Peter Walsh and Sally Seton obviously present the case for the development of the individual and the freedom of the spirit, which is set against the deadening influence of people like Hugh Whitbread and Sir William Bradshaw, and yet neither of them is approved of completely.

During the early years of her involvement with the group, Virginia read widely in English and European literature and gradually began to establish her own voice as an author. She began work on a novel in 1906, but it was never finished, and it was not until 1915 that her first novel, *The Voyage Out*, was published. The most important event of these years was her marriage to Leonard Woolf in 1912, for it was Leonard who would provide her with the stability necessary for her writing despite the continuing threat of madness. Like Virginia, Leonard was both a novelist and a critic. Though he had been at Cambridge with Thoby, Leonard's background was completely different from that of the Stephen family. He was Jewish (and therefore an outsider in England) and a life-long socialist. After his graduation from Cambridge he had made his career abroad as an administrator in Ceylon. However, during his long leave of 1911 he met Virginia, fell in love with her, and decided to abandon his career in order to marry because he realized that Virginia's health would suffer if she was obliged to live abroad. The marriage was never easy, though it was full of affection. For the rest of Virginia's life Leonard acted as companion and nurse, living constantly with the threat of madness if she over-exerted herself. Indeed, Richard Dalloway's solicitousness about his wife's health in *Mrs Dalloway* is in many ways similar to Leonard Woolf's concern for Virginia. Another similarity lies in Clarissa's feeling that she has failed her husband sexually. Virginia was wary of sexual contact and she fought shy of the physical side of marriage, even though she would have loved to have had children and was by all accounts extremely good with them. Leonard did not force the issue. Many years later Vita Sackville-West suggested that Virginia 'dislikes the possessiveness and love of domination in men. In fact she dislikes the quality of masculinity.' This element of Virginia's personality suffuses the characterization of Clarissa in the novel.

Because of his concern for Virginia, Leonard was careful to try and remove any stress from her life; he also wanted to offer her some therapy when she was recovering from her periods of madness. Consequently, in 1915 the Woolfs moved from central London to Hogarth House in Paradise Road, Richmond, on the outskirts of London, so that Virginia could escape from the bustle of the city. The therapy offered was the setting up of a hand operated printing press, known as the Hogarth Press, in 1917. At first the operation was small and laborious, with the Woolfs teaching themselves the mechanics of printing and distributing books. However, the enterprise was so successful that eventually they handed over the production side to professionals, retaining for themselves only the editing and business side of the press. One significance of the press was that it allowed them to promote new and unconventional literary works, and it was the Hogarth Press that first published T. S. Eliot's important volume *Poems 1919* and then in 1923 'The Waste Land', one of the most influential and revolutionary poems of the century. From Virginia's point of view, the press meant that she had complete control over the publication of her own novels and, with the exception of *Night and Day* (1919), all her books after the first were published with the Hogarth imprint.

The years after 1915 were also important because Virginia started to gain a reputation as a literary critic. In later years she produced her criticism in the form of volumes of essays, but between 1915 and 1922 she wrote 151 reviews for *The Times Literary Supplement* and a further 25 for the *New Statesman* and *Athenaeum*. Gradually, too, financial circumstances became easier, and in 1919 the Woolfs bought a weekend cottage called Monk's House in Rodmell, Sussex. Moreover, by 1924 Virginia was working hard to persuade Leonard that she was well enough to live in central London once again, particularly as she found the commuting to London a couple of times a week exhausting. Despite Leonard's reservations, Virginia won the day and they moved to 52

Tavistock Square in March 1924. The name of the press remained the same, however, acting as a reminder of their years in Richmond, though it was now run from the basement of their Bloomsbury home.

In 1922 Virginia's imagination began to work again on the portrait of a shallow and superficial society hostess called Mrs Dalloway, who had made a brief appearance in her first novel, *The Voyage Out*. At least part of the revival of interest in the character came about because of the death in October 1922 of Kitty Maxse, whom Virginia had used as her model. The original portrait had been rather unsympathetic and external, but in the intervening years Virginia's response had changed. The official view of Kitty's death was that she had fallen down a flight of stairs by accident, but Virginia remained convinced that she had committed suicide. The circumstances of the death lend *Mrs Dalloway* a series of images of the central character poised on a staircase, hovering between joy and despair; for Clarissa Dalloway, as for Kitty, there remains the possibility of a surrender to despair. However, as the writing of the novel progressed, the suicide theme became almost entirely focused in the character of Septimus Smith, though it is obvious that his death strikes a sympathetic chord within Clarissa when she hears of it.

Kitty's death, though formative, served merely to crystallize the response: on the one hand *Mrs Dalloway* is an affectionate tribute of 1922. During this time she was trying to come to terms with the complexity of her own response to the ruling classes. The memory of Kitty, the socialite who had tried to bring out the Stephen girls into high society (without success, it may be added!) during the early years of the century, offered her an imaginative starting point, because what she admired in Kitty was her ability to mix in this society without being compromised by it, thus losing her own values and integrity. The novel reflects the ambiguity of Virginia's response: on the one hand *Mrs Dalloway* is an affectionate tribute to a friend; on the other it is a savage attack upon a society and upon a woman whom she dismissed in her diary as being 'tinselly' and not worth bothering about. Quentin Bell has suggested that Virginia was a 'romantic snob' throughout her life, and that she was fascinated by the ruling classes despite her dismissal of them at times. *Mrs Dalloway* seems to bear out his theory.

Though we must never forget that art transforms experience rather than merely reflecting it, two other biographical issues are worth raising. The first centres on Septimus Smith's madness in the novel, for it is obvious that Virginia Woolf was calling upon her own experience here. Indeed, her diary for June 19, 1923 records that 'the mad part tries me so much, makes my mind squirt so badly that I can hardly face spending the next weeks at it'. From this we can see the pain that such writing caused her. More particularly still, the description of Dr Holmes and Sir William Bradshaw and the rest cure that they prescibe is obviously distilled from Virginia's recollection of Sir George Savage and the other meddling consultants who had insisted on incarcerating her in a Twickenham nursing home well away from members of her family during the black periods of 1910, 1912 and 1915.

The second biographical connection centres on Clarissa's memory of her passionate attachment to Sally Seton which contrasts sharply with the cool non-sexual feelings which she has for her husband. The link with the Woolfs' marriage is obvious, but the theme also recalls Virginia's own attachment to a number of women. The first of them was Madge Vaughan, a friend of the Stephen family during the 1890s, and Virginia freely admitted to Vita Sackville-West in 1928 that Madge was Sally in *Mrs Dalloway*, recalling that Clarissa's excitement about Sally's arrival at Bourton (p. 32) was based on a specific memory of herself in a top room in the house at Hyde Park Gate saying: 'Madge is here; at this moment she is actually under this roof'. Virginia had a number of other deep friendships with women such as Violet Dickinson (from about 1902 to 1907) and with Vita Sackville-West and, though it is unlikely that these friendships were sexual, it is nonetheless true to say that they showed a desire to flee from the threatening male which Clarissa shows through her distant, non-sexual response to both her husband and Peter Walsh.

By October 1922 Virginia Woolf was starting to realize that her random thoughts were beginning to take shape, nothing that '*Mrs Dalloway* has branched into a book.' By this stage, too, she had focused the central themes: 'I adumbrate here a study of insanity and suicide; the world seen by the sane and the insane side by side.' Over the following months *The Hours* (as it was called at this stage) continued to evolve slowly, and in July 1923 Virginia Woolf noted: 'In this book I have almost too many ideas. I want to give life and death, sanity and insanity; I want to criticize the social system and show it at work, at its most intense. But here I may be posing.' The precise technique of the novel continued to cause trouble, however, and it was not until October 1923 that she felt able to comment on it: 'Of course, I've only been feeling my way into it – up till last August anyhow. It took me a year's groping to discover what I call my tunnelling process, by which I tell the past by instalments as I have need of it. This is my primary discovery so far.'

During the following months she made reasonable though at times slow progress, and by May 1924 she was promising herself that she would finish both *The Hours* and a volume of essays during the course of the summer so that they could both appear early in 1925. As the summer progressed, elation was often followed by intense depressions. On 2 August, for example, she recorded that she was 'at a low ebb with my book – the death of Septimus – and I begin to count myself as a failure'. It was in moods such as this that she would take up the routine business of running the Hogarth Press with enthusiasm, recognizing that 'it entirely prevents brooding; and gives me something to fall back on'. As always when deeply involved in a book, she lived in fear of re-reading what she had written and discovering it to be 'pale'. Her various diary entries also make it plain that the writing did not come easily. As early as 1922 she complained: 'I am laboriously dredging my mind for *Mrs Dalloway* and bringing up light buckets.' And in late 1923 she considered herself lucky if she wrote even fifty words in a morning. Even towards the end she longed for greater ease, complaining in August 1924 that she was 'hacking at this miserable 200 words a day'. However, by October the novel's first draft was complete, and she felt that she could congratulate herself on having finished without lapsing into illness: 'I felt glad to be quit of it, yet fresher in the head; with less I mean of the usual feeling that I've shaved through and just kept my feet on the tight-rope.' Work on revision now began, with Virginia attempting to pull the disparate elements of the novel together as she re-typed it. As she worked she became conscious of the novel as indicative of her innermost self for, as she says in her diary for December 13, 1924, 'it seems to leave me plunged deep in the richest state of my mind'. By January 1925 the novel was at the proof stage, and it was finally published in May, shortly after *The Common Reader*, Virginia Woolf's first volume of critical essays. To her delight, *Mrs Dalloway* seemed much more instantly popular than the previous novels, with 1530 copies of the original edition of 2000 being sold by July.

Buoyed up by the success of *Mrs Dalloway*, Virginia Woolf found a new fluency in her writing during the next few years as she tackled her even more experimental novels *To the Lighthouse* (1927) and *The Waves* (1931), both of which used stylistic devices as a means of emphasizing the workings of the consciousness and consequently placed little emphasis on the novel as a means of telling a story. By the end of the 1920s her fame both as a novelist and a literary critic was spreading. To some she was the loathsome epitome of all that was vacuous and trivial in the Bloomsbury group; to others she was an uncompromising artist and a champion of women's rights, particularly after the publication of her book *A Room of One's Own* in 1928, which discussed the role of women in society. Widespread acclaim for herself did not appeal to her, however, because she felt that she wanted to cultivate a public rather than a personal voice with which she could address some of the problems which confronted the nation during the troubled thirties.

During these years the Woolfs enjoyed an increasingly happy marriage and spent more time at Monk's House, retreating there permanently once war with Germany became inevitable in 1939. For the most part they lived a quiet and ordered existence. Public tributes were offered in the form of honorary degrees from many universities, but all of them were refused. The most tempting offer came from Cambridge which invited her to give the Clark Lectures for 1933, a series which her father had given fifty years before. She declined, but was at the same time deeply flattered, noting: 'father would have blushed with pleasure could I have told him 30 years ago, that his daughter – my poor little Ginny – was to be asked to succeed him'.

The happiness of the 1930s was marred by the deaths of a number of close friends such as Lytton Strachey and Roger Fry. Particularly after the death of her nephew Julian Bell in the Spanish Civil War, Virginia Woolf became increasingly obsessed with her family and her past again. She had always aimed to write an autobiography, and to that end she had written diaries since 1917; however, the material had a severely depressing effect on her. Gradually the coming cataclysm of the Second World War together with her desire to dredge up the past reacted upon her sanity. Although she had not had one of her mad fits since the crisis of 1915, in January 1941 she found herself surrendering to the self-absorption which had preceded her other attacks. During the next couple of months it became apparent to Leonard that she was not well, though Virginia would not admit it because of the nature of her illness and because she feared a repetition of the rest cure which had been imposed upon her before. By the time that a decision had been made about how to nurse her it was too late: on the morning of 28 March she walked out to her studio in the garden at Monk's House, wrote letters to Leonard and to Vanessa – the two people whom she cared for most – and then committed suicide by carefully placing a stone in her coat pocket before walking into the river.

2 SUMMARIES AND CRITICAL COMMENTARY

2.1 INTRODUCTION

This guide has been prepared using the 1976 Grafton paperback edition of *Mrs Dalloway*. Each section of the novel is treated as a chapter, but in order to make the plot clearer, there are subdivisions which will take you through episode by episode. It is important to notice, though, that the Grafton edition differs from the original Hogarth (1925) edition in one respect: there should be a space between the bottom of page 51 and the top of page 52. As Woolf intended to include the space, the guide takes account of it.

Plot

Although *Mrs Dalloway* is a rather forbidding novel when approached for the first time, the plot is, in fact, extremely straightforward. Mrs Clarissa Dalloway, the middle-aged, convalescent wife of Richard Dalloway, a Member of Parliament, is to hold an important party on a June night in 1923. One thread of the novel follows her thoughts and actions as she moves through the day making her preparations. The reader is also asked to see her from other people's points of view, ranging from family and close friends through to those who merely see her from a distance in the street. The most complex response comes from Peter Walsh, newly returned from India (which was still at that stage part of the British Empire) to arrange his marriage to Daisy, currently the wife of a Major who is serving in the British army in India. Peter is deeply critical of the way that Clarissa has given herself over entirely to her husband and to high society; and yet as someone who never quite recovered from loving her and being rejected, he retains an affectionate and indulgent attitude towards her.

A stark contrast to the lives, concerns and pretension of those who inhabit the upper-middle, governing class is provided by the story of Septimus Smith, a self-educated war veteran, and his Italian wife Lucrezia (usually called Rezia in the novel). The events of their day are paralleled with those of Clarissa and her circle, but it is not until the evening that the two worlds truly overlap when Sir William Bradshaw, a physician, talks to Richard Dalloway about the suicide of Septimus, who is one of his patients. Although England has largely recovered from the horror of the First World War (1914–18), Septimus remains a victim because he still suffers from shell-shock which pushes him into periods of madness in which he has visions and thinks that he sees his friend Evans who was killed during the war. He is one of the 'forgotten heroes' ignored by society now that they have done their duty. During the day Rezia, desperately alone because in a foreign country and unable to communicate with her husband, takes him to see Sir William, a specialist in nervous diseases. However, Sir William is deeply unperceptive and, if anything, he makes matters worse because his well-meaning concern, like that of his colleague Dr Holmes, is seen as a threat by Septimus. Later in the day Dr Holmes calls on the Smiths at their lodgings in Bloomsbury, with the intention of having Septimus taken to a mental home. Septimus, worried that everyone is trying to pry into his soul, throws himself out of the window to his death.

The novel ends with Mrs Dalloway's party. The news of Septimus's death breaks in upon Clarissa's gaiety. But even though she is disturbed, she decides not to let her own feelings subdue the mood of her guests. By the end, her old friend Peter Walsh sees her in a new way, though she still remains an enigma.

Chronology

During the novel Woolf makes a great deal of play with the idea that there are two different sorts of time: chronological and internal (i.e. a character's ability to range backwards and forwards through the use of memory and to become oblivious to what is going on in the outside world). The first of these is measured by the chiming of clocks throughout the novel. From the reader's point of view these small reminders help to make sense of the novel's structure by showing that some scenes in the novel are, in fact, going on at the same time. The table below should help you to sort out this aspect of the novel.

Pages	Events	Time
5–15	Clarissa's shopping trip	10:00–11:00 am
15–21	Londoners, including Clarissa and the Smiths, observe the unidentified car and the aeroplane	10:00–11:00 am
21–5	Septimus and Rezia in Regent's Park. His first hallucination	10:30–11:00 am
25–7	London observed by minor characters	10:45–11:00 am
27–37	Clarissa at home	11:00 am onwards
37–44	Peter's visit to Clarissa	After 11:00 am
44–51	Peter's walk to Regent's Park	11:15 am
52–3	Peter's dream	11:45? am
53–9	Peter's memories of Bourton	Just before noon
59–64	Smith's conversation; Septimus's vision	11:40 am onwards
	Septimus observed by Peter	11:45 am
64–72	Peter's thoughts about Clarissa, Bourton and his own life. Encounter with old woman on leaving the park	after 11:45 am
72–84	Smiths leave the park. Septimus's history	just before noon
84–91	Smiths' consultation with Sir William Bradshaw	noon–12:45 pm
91–100	Lady Bruton's lunch for Richard Dalloway and Hugh Whitbread	1:30–3:00 pm
100–7	Richard Dalloway's walk home Richard and Clarissa at home	2:45–3:00 pm
107–13	Clarissa's thoughts about Miss Kilman	Before 3:30 pm
113–9	Miss Kilman and Elizabeth Dalloway shopping and tea	After 3:30 pm
119–24	Elizabeth's bus ride	After 4:00 pm

124–34	Smiths at home. Dr Holmes's visit Septimus's suicide	6:00 pm
134–46	Peter's thoughts and preparations for the party	After 6:00 pm
146–62	The party from various viewpoints	? to 3:00 am
162–5	Clarissa's withdrawal and return	? to 2:30 am
165–72	Conversation of Peter and Sally	? to 3:00 am

2.2 – 12 SUMMARIES AND COMMENTARIES

2.2 Pp. 5–14

We are immediately introduced to the central character of the novel. One morning in June 1923 Mrs Clarissa Dalloway leaves her home in Westminster to buy flowers for the party she is to hold in the evening. The weather reminds her of the time when she was eighteen and staying at Bourton, a country house. She looks back on her young self on the verge of adult life ('feeling as she did, standing there at the open window, that something awful was about to happen'). She also recalls that Peter Walsh, who was there at that time, is due back from his term of duty in India. Already we see Woolf trying to show us how a mind works by fluttering from topic to topic with its own logic which is only vaguely related to external factors. And, though the author is obliged to present thoughts in order, she intends us to recognize that the mind works on many different levels simultaneously.

As Clarissa heads towards the florists, her mind is full of thoughts about her life in Westminster over the last twenty years and the new spirit of hopefulness which now dominates post-war Britain. Scrope Purvis, a neighbour, gives us an external, masculine view of Clarissa by noting to himself that she is 'charming' and with 'a touch of the bird about her'. However, he has also hit upon one of the central complexities of her character when he observes that she is at the same time 'upright' for this hints at the rigidity of character and behaviour that others also see in Clarissa. Indeed, we see it ourselves almost immediately because Woolf draws particular attention to Clarissa's admiration of Lady Bexborough who showed typical British courage during the war when she opened a bazaar while at the same time holding the telegram which informed her that her son had been killed.

Walking on through St James's Park, Clarissa hears Big Ben, the clock on the Houses of Parliament, striking. As we will see, the passing of time haunts the major characters throughout the novel. In Clarissa's case, she tries to escape from time and its 'leaden circles' by immersing herself in the glories of the present moment: 'life; London; this moment of June'. During the course of her walk, Clarissa meets Hugh Whitbread (based on George Duckworth, Woolf's half-brother), an old friend who has a job at the royal court. Clarissa carries on a conversation about Hugh's wife Evelyn, but at the same time she is also thinking about her hat and the way that whenever she meets Hugh she always feels like a schoolgirl once again. The meeting prompts further thought about Peter, whom Hugh never liked. When they were young Peter criticized Hugh for being a typical product of the English upper classes – well trained and cultured but utterly incapable of feeling sympathy for other people. And while Clarissa has never quite agreed with Peter's analysis, she has always recognized that he, rather than Hugh, was 'adorable to walk with on a morning like this'.

Retreating further into herself, Clarissa reflects upon Peter's concern with art and philosophical speculation which made him uncompromising in his condemnation of her marriage to Richard Dalloway who was, in Peter's eyes, like Hugh. Although she has shaken off his criticism of her as having the 'makings of a perfect hostess', there is an element of truth in it because we see Clarissa as predominantly concerned – from an outsider's point of view anyway – with trivia, and later she is unwilling to allow her own feelings about Septimus Smith's death to mar the mood of the guests at her party. As she continues her walk she speculates about what it would have been like had she married Peter Walsh and concludes that he would have destroyed her because he would have allowed her no privacy. With him 'everything had to be shared; everything gone into. And it was intolerable.' She recalls too the moment by the fountain in the garden at Bourton when she broke off with Peter, while recognizing at the same time that she has retained affection for him.

Standing now at the gates of St James's Park, she observes the traffic on Piccadilly and thinks about the nature of human personality and how impossible it is to know another person or, indeed, herself ('and she would not say of Peter, she would not say of herself, I am this, I am that'). Because of this impossibility, she recognizes that everyone is essentially alone and isolated. Her stance here contrasts with the earlier idea that she wanted to retain her inner privacy from Peter's prying nature, and it suggests that her views about the matter are ambiguous. Clarissa's sense of loneliness ('She had a perpetual sense . . . of being out, out, far to sea and alone') is only alleviated by her joy in the present ('what she loved was this, here, now') which allows her to put aside thoughts of death temporarily.

Moving on down Piccadilly, Clarissa looks in at the window of Hatchards the bookshop for something to take to Hugh Whitbread's wife Evelyn, who is in a nursing home. As she does so she thinks back on a more innocent and hopeful age (a 'white dawn in the country') shared by her group of friends before the war. The thought introduces a new theme to the novel because the reader is aware that Woolf intends the war to act as a shadow over the book through the character of Septimus Smith: the gaiety which is everywhere apparent in the novel's descriptions of London is fragile and melancholic because the whole society has lost its innocence. Enjoyment can only be had by ignoring (as society does with Septimus) reality. Clarissa thinks once again about Lady Bexborough's heroism at the bazaar, seeing the incident as symbolic of the disparity between inner and outer, private grief and public responsibility. While the reader is obviously supposed to sympathize to an extent, the nature of the event, a mere bazaar, trivializes the idea of heroism and makes us aware of Clarissa's limited appreciation of the reality of war for those who actually had to fight.

Clarissa now questions her motives for wanting to go and visit Evelyn Whitbread, realizing that she is doing so because she wants to be liked rather than because she has any feeling for Evelyn. Further reflection leads her on to think how she would model herself on Lady Bexborough if she had her life again. Clarissa responds to Lady Bexborough's apparent integrity and self-control, but the reader knows that this is only a subjective impression and that the reality might be somewhat different. Attention is drawn to Clarissa's attempts to see herself in all her various roles: as a private person; as a mother; and as Mrs Richard Dalloway, an extension of her husband. Wandering in the crowd deprives her of all these identities; she seems to be merely part of the flow around her. As she wanders on up Bond Street she thinks once more of the consolations of the present moment ('That is all') because she has no faith in anything beyond time and death. Prompted by her earlier reflections on motherhood, her thoughts turn to Elizabeth, her daughter, who seems unwilling to adopt her mother's values. Clarissa is distressed because her faith in surface appearance (symbolized by the gloves and shoes) is not shared. Once again the reader sees her limitations. Clarissa is also distressed by Elizabeth's fondness for Miss Kilman, an ex-schoolmistress turned Christian evangelist who, because of her poverty, her faith, and her disdain of the way that the Dalloways live, makes Clarissa feel uneasy.

Clarissa never likes to face up to her darker emotions such as her ability to hate. Moreover, she wants to ignore the way that her recent illness has made her face her own inevitable death. She therefore dismisses all deeper thoughts about the significance of her life as 'Nonsense, nonsense,' placing her faith instead in 'beauty, in friendship, in being well, in being loved and making her home delightful' (p. 13). The choosing of the flowers acts, therefore, as a means of evading unpleasant thoughts. However, the reader is made aware of the reality by Miss Pym's external view, for she sees Clarissa as 'older, this year'. While Clarissa is in the shop she hears the backfiring of a car in the street.

2.3 Pp. 14–27

We are already aware of how Woolf is interested in the way that people search for significance in their lives, and the backfiring of a car in the street broadens out the theme, because the passers-by assume that it must contain someone of importance. They feel that close proximity to figures of authority (which is what Clarissa wants with the Prime Minister later) gives them a sense of order in the world which is otherwise missing.

An external event also gives Woolf the opportunity to move us outside the shop and into the minds of Septimus Smith and his wife who stop to watch the car which has paused outside Mulberry's. Septimus (who is described as looking 'beak-nosed' and therefore connected to Clarissa who has been described as 'bird-like') feels that the attention of all the passers-by is focused on him. Whereas Clarissa sees joy in the present moment, he can only see cause for depression and insecurity. Rezia is deeply protective towards him, and yet also embarrassed about his behaviour in public, feeling irrationally that 'People must notice; people must see'. Woolf is obviously contrasting Septimus's lack of an acceptable public self to the controlled exterior which Clarissa presents to observers.

Speculation by the crowd about who is in the car grows, but their suspicions about the occupant's identity show more about the crowd's differing preoccupations than about reality. For Clarissa, now leaving Mulberry's, it seems probable that the Queen is being delayed. This suggestion shows us once again that Clarissa is obsessed with rank, position, and the continuity of history which allows her to feel safe. She longs for the sense of significance that mixing with 'society' will confer upon her at her party ('She stiffened a little; so she would stand at the top of her stairs'). The moment is shared unknowingly with Sir John Brockhurst (an ageing judge), with the flower woman Moll Pratt, and with various others from all levels of society, thus showing how people are unknowingly connected.

At the same time, a small crowd has gathered outside Buckingham Palace in the hope of seeing one of the Royal family. The hope adds glamour and a sense of purpose to their otherwise uneventful lives. Suddenly the people in Bond Street and those outside the Palace are connected by the sight of an aeroplane sky-writing above them. For most of the spectators the writing is merely an advertisement, but for Septimus, now sitting in Regent's Park, it is a message from another world. Suddenly the physical world takes on a new and almost unbearable liveliness to Septimus: it seems to have a life of its own. He is forced to shut his eyes. His utter self-absorption terrifies Rezia. Despite reassurances from Dr Holmes, she is convinced that Septimus is deranged. Woolf draws attention to the way in which the Smiths have become estranged from each other within marriage: communication between the two has come to an end, despite their affection for each other.

We move inside Rezia's mind. Her being alone in a foreign country effectively symbolizes the theme of isolation hinted at in all the married relationships in the book. For her, recollections of life in Italy point out the limitations of England where the people are 'half alive'. These thoughts force a mood of bleak loneliness upon her ('I am alone; I am alone'). Meanwhile, Septimus remains transfixed, talking to himself and writing down what is revealed on the backs of envelopes. He has lost all interest in presenting a public self to the world which is at odds with his inner fantasies; instead he is obsessively concerned with communicating his vision which, sadly, is meaningless. Rezia tries to move Septimus away from the public gaze, partly through embarrassment and partly because of her love for him which means that she does not want others to mock. At the same time she tries to follow Dr Holmes's advice to interest him in the outside world as a means of drawing him out of himself. Her attempts are unsuccessful. In his fantasies, Septimus sees himself as being a saviour destined to renew society through his death. Like Christ, another 'eternal sufferer' on mankind's behalf, he is deeply unwilling to embrace his fate. Woolf shows us – and we can be sure that she was writing out of her own experience – the utter isolation of madness here. Ironically, Septimus's visions rightly suggest to him that it is the external world which is corrupt. The visions distort the 'sane' world perceived by the other characters, but at the same time they have a truth of their own. As we will see later, Septimus is right to mistrust people like Holmes who have lost all connection with their own sense of compassion and feeling.

A further example of isolation is now seen in the brief portrait of Maisie Johnson, newly arrived from Edinburgh to take up a position in her uncle's house. She asks the Smiths the way to Regent's Park underground station and is made homesick by their odd behaviour, which she takes as typical of Londoners. Maisie is observed by an older woman, Mrs Dempster, who is thinking about her own life, the failure of her marriage and her son who drinks. Like Clarissa, she speculates about how life might have been different. Although she is happy with her lot, she still longs for romance in life. Her desire for 'Pity, for the loss of roses' makes explicit the connection between her and Clarissa. Both have given themselves to life; both have been hurt. As with the Dalloways' and the Smiths' marriages, we are obviously meant to respond to the loss of innocence which marriage brings.

Mrs Dempster sees the plane flying overhead, and it becomes for her, as for Mr Bentley a groundsman down the river at Greenwich, a symbol of freedom and escape; 'an aspiration . . . a symbol of man's soul; of his determination . . . to get outside his body'. Meanwhile, another man, unnamed and unemployed, notices the plane just before he enters St Paul's Cathedral. For him, the cathedral seems to offer significance and connection in life because it enables him to feel the power of history. Like Clarissa on the opening page of the book speculating about the pleasures and responsibilities of throwing herself wholeheartedly into life, he stands on a threshold wondering whether or not to commit himself to something and asking 'why not enter in?' As with many of the novel's characters, he is searching for a sense of direction in life.

2.4   **Pp. 27–44**

(a)   **Beginning to 'She had not read his letter' (p. 37)**

As she arrives home, Clarissa wonders what everyone is looking at in the sky. She passes into the hall of the house, treasuring the comfort, familiarity and sense of identity which her home offers. The tranquillity of her mood is broken by Lucy's news that Mr Dalloway will be lunching with Lady Bruton. Clarissa is upset, though not entirely because she has been snubbed. It is rather that Lady Bruton, an old lady who has devoted herself to giving 'amusing' parties, is a version of Clarissa herself, for she sees in Lady Bruton the emptiness of her own life and of 'the dwindling of life; how year by year her share was sliced'. As Clarissa retreats upstairs to her attic bedroom, we are suddenly made aware of one of Clarissa's inner contradictions. She feels a joyful anticipation when she is about to act as a hostess, but at the same time social events are also perceived as threatening to the inner sense of identity: they are a sea which might engulf her. Consequently, Clarissa needs both sociability and the intense privacy of her own room if she is to retain a full sense of her identity. The attic room which she has occupied since her illness so that Richard will not wake her when he comes in from late sittings of Parliament, symbolizes both her desire for privacy and also her isolation. It serves to remind her of her loneliness and her lack of fulfilment, that 'there was an emptiness about the heart of life'.

It is here that a reader becomes aware of her unwillingness to surrender her inner privacy to another. Although she has a daughter, she has never truly given her whole self to Richard. By shying away from her sexual nature she has retained a virginity of the soul. While she is on her way upstairs she is seen as being 'Like a nun withdrawing.' And slightly later her own thoughts wistfully point out that 'she could not dispel a virginity preserved through childbirth which clung to her like a sheet'. In contrast, Clarissa recalls how occasionally when she has been taken into another woman's confidence she has felt the closeness which she knows ought to exist between a man and his wife. She has not, however, had the experience of 'illumination', of 'an inner meaning almost expressed' within her own marriage. There is affection and amusement and also a need for each other, but there is no desire to explore each other deeply. This is what Clarissa has deliberately chosen, but in doing so she has limited herself. Of course there was an alternative: but Woolf intends us to see that the marriage with Peter Walsh would have been equally limiting, though in a different way.

Clarissa's mind now moves on to think about how she once loved Sally Seton. The recollection of having been attracted to someone of her own sex causes her great embarrassment. Yet at the same time she remembers the passion as having had great purity and intensity. For once in her life she could have given herself to someone completely. Sally's kiss is recalled as having caused feelings which Clarissa has never felt since. Though Sally's influence on Clarissa caused her to be interested in socialism and art, what she responded to most was Sally's lack of formality, symbolized still in her mind by Sally's dash for the bathroom with no clothes on. Though the thoughts of love have long disappeared, Clarissa can still recall being transfixed by her passion for Sally and her feeling of intense hatred towards Peter for having interrupted their kiss in the garden at Bourton. As elsewhere, Clarissa shies back from men, valuing instead the companionship of her own sex.

The memory of Peter's behaviour on that occasion is countered by a further assessment of him. Clarissa now realizes how much he helped to shape her whole attitude towards life. These thoughts make her feel old. She longs to escape the 'icy claws' of time by throwing herself into the joys of the present. But at the same time she recognizes that she cannot escape: the present – 'this June morning' – contains within it the process of her ageing ('the pressure of all the other mornings').

As she looks into the mirror she ponders the nature of human personality and the disparity between her public and her private self. She recognizes that she prepares herself in a certain way when she is to meet others. To them she seems to be a diamond which is hard and unchanging; to herself the diamond is multi-faceted and deeply flawed by 'faults, jealousies, vanities, suspicion'. Rather than surrender to these thoughts, Clarissa resolves to keep herself busy by mending the dress that she is to wear in the evening. As always, preparations for a party console her and keep her from examining herself too closely. As she leaves the room, however, she is aware of having to assemble her public personality ('that diamond shape, that single person') so that she can appear to others to be in control of herself.

While she has been upstairs, Lucy has been arranging ornaments in the drawing room and thinking about Clarissa and the party. Clarissa is seen as a sympathetic though demanding mistress who inspires affection from her servants by allowing them to stay out late when they go to the theatre and by complimenting them on their efforts. Lucy retires, leaving Clarissa to get on with her mending. Clarissa thinks about her dressmaker, whom she has never managed to visit since she retired to the suburbs. Woolf is perhaps hinting gently that her good intentions are rather insincere. As she sits absorbed in her sewing, which gives her a great sense of peace of mind, she is suddenly interrupted by a ringing at the front door. Peter Walsh, newly arrived from India, presses past Lucy, assuming that Clarissa will be delighted to see him. Clarissa meanwhile, 'like a virgin protecting chastity,' hastens to hide her dress, feeling that her privacy has been violated. She is pleased to see Peter, but his behaviour reminds her of her reason for not marrying him.

(b) From ' "And how are you?" ' (p. 37) to 'as Peter Walsh shut the door' (p. 44)

Peter at once notices that Clarissa has aged since he last saw her. He is slightly embarrassed in her presence and he resolves not to tell her about his marriage plans. Meanwhile, Clarissa notes that he is still the same, even down to his annoying habit of fingering his pocket-knife when he is slightly nervous. She feels that he is still critical of the life which she has chosen and consequently teases him by refusing to invite him to the party where she will, after all, be displaying the side of herself which he most dislikes. Despite his unspoken criticism of her complacency, Peter envies Clarissa the stability of her life. What he really wants from her is approval of what he is about to do, despite his longing to be independent of her.

As the two remember the past together they start to warm to each other. The barrier between them begins to dissolve. Prompted by Clarissa's memories of Bourton, Peter is suddenly caught up in the remembered grief which was a consequence of Clarissa's refusal to marry him. Peter suspects that she is manipulating the conversation so that she can keep her distance from him. While these thoughts are going through his head Clarissa reminds him of the lake at Bourton and becomes absorbed in her own memory of feeding the ducks with her parents when she was a small child. As the memory develops she finds herself imagining a scene in which she presents her life's achievements to her parents. Her bleak self-questioning about her success ('And what had she made of it?') is paralleled by Peter thinking similar thoughts about himself and contrasting his own lack of control over his life with the success, both material and spiritual, which the Dalloways have had. At the same time, however, he continues to detest their smugness, not realizing that Clarissa feels more than she can express. Even though he shows contempt for the values which Clarissa appears to endorse, her presence gives him a new perspective on his life (the same happens later when Clarissa's letter arrives at his hotel room) by making him aware of Daisy's limitations.

Externally their conversation gradually becomes a skirmish of egos, with Clarissa seeing herself as like a sleeping princess who has been vulnerable because unguarded. In order to maintain her individuality she has to think hard about the elements of her life – 'the things she liked; her husband; Elizabeth; her self, in short' – which Peter is excluded from. She cannot afford to let him threaten her inner self. Peter meanwhile is keen to convince her that he can manage perfectly well without her approval. However, his actions, particularly when he bursts into tears in front of her, betray his true feelings of insecurity and self-doubt. As Peter has been telling her about Daisy, Clarissa has been reflecting on his weaknesses. She sees him as a victim of his own insensitivity towards others. And yet at the same time she also finds his emotionality endearing, particularly when she compares it with her own lack of feeling. Peter's love for Daisy, though selfish, makes her aware once again of her own loneliness within marriage. For all her doubts about Peter, she feels that her life might have been more glamorous if she had married him. She longs to escape from the restrictions of her own life ('Take me with you Clarissa thought impulsively'). Peter attempts to get behind Clarissa's social façade to find out if she is truly happy, but before she can answer Elizabeth arrives. Peter leaves hastily, embarrassed by his behaviour and by his exclusion from Clarissa's present life. Her plea that he should remember her party serves to establish once again her independence from him.

2.5 Pp. 44–51

Peter finds himself in the street listening to the half hour strike. As he walks away down Victoria Street his mind is full of thoughts about love, his achievements in India of which Clarissa knows nothing, and motor cars. He has been offended by Clarissa's coldness, both towards himself and towards Elizabeth. He resents her conventionality and his own inability to keep things from her. As St Margaret's church clock strikes the half hour he remembers once again the pain of Clarissa's original refusal of him. The chime seems to him like a hostess who is never too forward and it becomes confused with his thoughts about Clarissa and her appearance at a party years before 'coming downstairs on the stroke of the hour in white.' As the bell's sound fades he recalls the passing of time and Clarissa's recent illness which acts as a reminder 'of death that surprised in the midst of life.' Unconsciously he is also thinking about the metaphorical death which he thinks has overtaken Clarissa. The reminder of death forces him to assess his own achievements once again, and particularly the socialist beliefs he held when young. As always, his attitude towards Clarissa is coloured by his knowledge of Richard Dalloway's 'set', which seems to him obsessed with trivia.

As these thoughts pass through his head a troop of soldiers marches past. Peter admires them for their ability to put their faith in something outside themselves, even though he distrusts militarism. They at least seem to have certain aims in life. Equally, the statues of various soldiers and statesmen which he sees in Whitehall, the centre of Britain's politics, remind him of his lack of success in public life. At the same time, he suddenly finds himself feeling liberated from the roles that others thrust upon him because no-one recognizes him in the street. Aware of the present moment as being full of infinite possibilities, he follows a girl down the street while at the same time imagining an encounter between them. Fairly obviously, he seeks consolation from his fantasies because he did not get it from his meeting with Clarissa. However, the girl's disappearance into a house forces him back into the real world and makes him recognize the power of the mind which seems to him to make up 'the better part of life'. Peter is presented here as being lonely and unfulfilled: as with many others in the novel the life of the mind dominates and communication with others has been abandoned. Although he thinks that he wants to stand by his old principles of sincerity and openness, Peter has unconsciously built barriers around himself. Both here and in his relationship with Daisy his true aim is to have someone flatter his image of himself without giving anything in return.

Having had his 'fun' Peter decides to walk for a while until it is time for him to go and see his lawyers about the divorce. Like Clarissa earlier, he enjoys the lack of identity that the anonymous city streets confer on him. And although he has been seen elsewhere as being contemptuous of the world of debutantes and the Dalloways, his feelings are ambiguous. As he walks on he feels proud of the 'civilization' which he sees around him. Arriving at Regent's Park, he remembers playing there when a child. He sits down on a bench and thinks once more about Clarissa and Elizabeth, tracing his dissatisfaction to Clarissa's possessiveness about her daughter ('There's my Elizabeth'), which he thinks is an attempt to dominate her.

2.6   Pp. 52–3

The nurse who sits at the other end of Peter Walsh's bench knitting gradually becomes incorporated into his dreams. We are meant to take the dream as being both particular to Peter and yet also an expression of the general internal human conflict between freedom and familiarity. Peter, like everyone else, is a 'solitary traveller' seeking a sense of significance in life. At times he thinks that there is nothing beyond the here and now, the present moment; but yet at the same time he is also aware of an unfocused longing, a desire for a cause or for a religious faith which will confer meaning on life. Peter's imagination transforms the nurse into a giant, thus hinting that perhaps Peter feels limited and threatened by women in their roles as wives and mothers. She seems to promise him an attractive escape from his tedious, mundane existence (just as the girl that he followed did), but it is soon obvious that the other world offered is in fact death, a disturbing unknown; the woman is in fact a siren who is luring him to destruction.

In contrast, Peter also dreams about the consolation which can be had within time and from 'ordinary things'. In this respect he is like Clarissa. His vision of himself as a hero returning in glory after a quest is empty, and he longs instead for an ideal housekeeper who will offer him comfort without his having to become involved. However, her question – ' "There is nothing more tonight, Sir?" ' – also carries with it the threat of life without a spiritual side. Peter is torn between the siren and the housekeeper, for both have their allure. However, neither offers true consolation. Peter is left with his longing to be loved and understood which neither the girl that he followed nor Clarissa supplied.

2.7 Pp. 53–9

Peter suddenly awakes from his sleep and finds himself concerned with 'The death of the soul', particularly with reference to Clarissa. He feels that the values of upper-class British society corrupt people's spontaneity and inner life. The thought soon becomes attached to a particular memory of Clarissa at Bourton many years before. He recalls Clarissa's mockery of a visiting servant girl and how it suddenly changed to moral affront when Sally revealed that the girl had had an illegitimate child. In that moment, Peter felt that he had seen all that Clarissa would become in middle age: 'timid; hard; arrogant; prudish.' He contrasts Clarissa's attitude to the girl with Sally's desire to shock. He remembers also that Clarissa obviously felt embarrassed by her over-reaction and later fussed over her dog in front of him so that he would see her capacity for affection and spontaneity. Nonetheless, he had seen the limitation – 'this coldness, this woodenness... an impenetrability' – which would place a barrier between them.

He recalls that it was in the evening of this same day that she first met Richard. From the start Peter recognised that she would marry him because he offered her a conventional, safe existence. What he still fails to recognize, however, is that behind the surface of the 'perfect hostess' (which was his taunt to her on this occasion), there is a woman who can neither allow herself to be taken over by someone else nor face the implications of her intuitions and feelings. In this respect he greatly misunderstands Clarissa.

Looking back once again to the evening at Bourton, he remembers both his feeling of loneliness when he was left behind when the others went on a boating expedition and the sudden joy when Clarissa suddenly came to rescue him from a dull conversation with Miss Parry. The memory causes him to reflect upon his own limitations and, in particular, his lack of self-restraint when talking to Clarissa which made him seem 'absurd' to her. Peter also recalls the moment at which he recognized that his instinct about Richard was right because Clarissa would no longer joke about Richard's name. Finally, he thinks about Clarissa's rejection of him by the fountain at Bourton. For him the way that Clarissa dealt with the situation which he had brought about was proof that she was 'like iron, like flint, rigid up the backbone'.

During this series of Peter's memories we are given the whole of the history of the courtship between Clarissa and Richard. Peter's prejudice against Richard and the values which he represents are made absolutely explicit. Amongst other things, Woolf intends us to note how minute particulars of someone's behaviour can give clues about their inner thoughts.

2.8 Pp.59–84

(a) **Beginning to 'the quarter to twelve' (p. 64)**

Peter gradually starts to take notice of the outside world again in an effort to cheer himself up. He is amused by little Elsie Mitchell who is carrying pebbles to her nurse. Meanwhile, Rezia has left Septimus talking to his imaginary friend and now walks by herself, lonely and isolated. For a moment the worlds of the Dalloways and the Smiths coincide, though none of the characters realize it: Elsie runs into Rezia by accident, bursts into tears, and is then comforted by the nurse and by Peter, who allows her to see his watch. Rezia, like Peter earlier, is absorbed in her own thoughts and hardly pays attention to what is going on around her. She thinks about her own sacrifices and about the progress of Septimus's madness. She has witnessed Septimus's delayed reaction to the war and his gradual withdrawal from the world. Despite Dr Holmes's assurances that there is nothing wrong – a view which tells us more about Holmes than about Septimus – Rezia remains full of foreboding because of Septimus's talk about suicide. Our attention is drawn to Septimus's view that everyone lies to everyone else because Woolf wants us to see that this mad vision has some truth: it is an extreme version of the novel's idea that we present a 'public' self to the world.

When Rezia returns to Septimus she explains why she no longer wears her wedding ring. Septimus takes her gesture as being symbolic of his liberation from marriage. He starts to think about how his visions can be communicated to people in authority. Deprived of the ability to influence the world when sane, his fantasies give him an illusion of power and he sees himself as 'the lord of men'. His thoughts are interrupted by the appearance of a small dog which changes into a man before his eyes. All the external influences on Septimus such as the traffic and the trees suddenly take on a ghastly supernatural vividness because of his madness. Septimus remains remote from the world ('high on his rock') and yet at the same time, like Clarissa, he is acutely aware of beauty and 'something tremendous about to happen' (an echo of Clarissa's 'something awful was about to happen'). While Rezia is talking to him, Septimus suddenly sees a man in grey approaching him and he assumes that it must be Evans bringing him a message, though it is in fact Peter Walsh. As the clock strikes a quarter to twelve the reader is acutely aware of the enormous distance between the Smiths. The similarity between Clarissa and Septimus has been explicitly made, for both seek a sense of meaning and significance in life.

(b) From 'And that is being young' (p. 64) to 'at the crossing' (p.72)

As Peter walks past the Smiths on his way out of the park he assumes that he is witnessing a lovers' quarrel. He thinks about the various ways in which England has changed during his absence and particularly the way that many formerly taboo subjects are now openly talked about. Thoughts about the increasing freedom of women lead him naturally on to reflections about Sally Seton and her desire to live spontaneously, ignoring social pressure. Peter values Sally for her attempt to 'get hold of things by the right end anyhow.' In particular, he recalls that she was an ally at Bourton because she could see through the social veneer of 'that ancient lot', epitomized by the Whitbreads and the Dalloways, who governed Britain without truly caring about other people. To Sally these people were contemptible because they 'read nothing, thought nothing, felt nothing'. Peter's continuing dislike for the ruling classes comes through in his resentment of Hugh who is, after all, merely descended from 'Respectable tradespeople.' To him, Hugh's love of his job at court, his marriage to the Honourable Evelyn, and his passion for collecting antiques are all typical of a society which treasures the superficial. His dislike is further intensified by the recollection that he depends on Richard and Hugh to find him a job. Richard is spared some of Peter's resentment because he seems to care for Clarissa. Nonetheless, Peter sees him as intellectually limited because of his prudish attitude towards art. A further memory of Bourton now emerges in which Sally pleaded with him to 'save' Clarissa from the people who would unconsciously 'stifle her soul'. Despite his reservations about what happened to Clarissa subsequently, Peter is still able to warm to her fine sense of judgement about people. Moreover, he confirms for us Clarissa's own thought that her presence gives people a sense of fulfilment because she has a gift for 'making a world of her own wherever she happened to be'. The passage also illuminates something of the complexity of Peter's attitude towards her.

Peter tears himself away from his memories, determined not to allow thoughts about Clarissa to influence his present actions ('He was not in love with her any more!'). Once again he emphasizes her limitations to himself, criticizing her because 'she was worldly; cared too much for rank and society and getting on in the world' and is therefore, like Lady Bexborough, 'rigid' and unwilling to think for herself. Despite his reservations, Peter retains an admiration for Clarissa's determination not to be beaten into submission by life. He traces her philosophy to the moment when she saw her sister crushed by a tree and resolved that she could not believe in a benevolent power ruling the world. Her way of fighting the forces of anarchy has been to treasure life and to answer its malevolence with lady-like, decent behaviour. The philosophy is limited, but we have already witnessed it as a real force in Clarissa's inner life. Indeed, Lyndall Gordon has noted that Woolf felt much the same way because she inherited from her mother 'the Victorian agnostic's sense of futility balanced by solicitude'. Peter acknowledges that Clarissa's life is conventional, and yet at the same time he admires her for her ability to fulfil herself through other people, even though it will ultimately corrupt her. In contrast, he attempts to delude himself that he can manage perfectly well without other people, though it is obvious that this is merely because he fears rejection. It seems that although he does not love Daisy he intends to marry her because she flatters his inner self without threatening it. As Clarissa suspected, he wants to possess Daisy merely for selfish reasons. His cynicism about marital relationships parallels that of Septimus who married Rezia in the hope that he would be able to recover the ability to feel by having a focus for his emotions.

Peter's feelings of distance from Clarissa have been compromised by his tears in front of her that morning which showed that he still relies on her. Ironically he, like Clarissa, needs to retain an independent central core. His thoughts present the central paradox of his relationship with Clarissa: disillusionment and bitterness about her treatment of him (he sees her as 'cold as an icicle') is balanced against his view of her as an indispensable bringer of comfort, security and perspective to his life.

By now he has reached the gates of the park. The interview with the lawyers and his indecision about Daisy have been at the back of his mind, but now he must make a decision. He is both literally and metaphorically 'at the crossing.'

(c)   From 'A sound interrupted him' (p.72) to 'Dr Holmes, looking not quite so kind'

Peter's thoughts are interrupted by the strange singing of a woman who sits outside the underground railway station. In his mind she becomes a mythical figure who represents woman's eternal faithfulness to man, despite the disillusioning passage of time. And yet the experience of the woman in some 'primeval May' has merely left her shrivelled and lonely. Peter unconsciously seeks to compare the woman to Clarissa, seeing her as a tragic figure because of her rejection of him. Indeed, the moment when Peter presses a shilling into the woman's hand exactly parallels Clarissa's compassionate grasping of his hand during their meeting (p. 43). Once again we notice that Peter fantasizes about a woman's need for him as a means of compensating for his bitterness.

As the Smiths leave the park, they too see the old woman. Rezia is filled with deep sympathy for her because she recognizes in the woman some of her own loneliness. Rezia admires the woman's ability to sing despite adversity. Once again we see how different characters interpret external events according to their inner preoccupations. As always external 'reality' is seen as being entirely constructed from people's subjective perceptions.

The woman's song causes an irrational feeling of well-being in Rezia. She is suddenly convinced that Sir William Bradshaw will be able to cure Septimus. The Smiths walk away from the park towards Sir William's consulting rooms in Harley Street. As they are walking, Woolf presents us with an external view of them as being unassuming folk who fade into the crowd with no one suspecting their inner turmoil. During the next few pages Septimus's story is conventionally told so that we can trace the course of his illness up to the present moment. He is revealed as being typical of many young men who try to achieve fame and fortune by moving to London but are eventually swallowed up by the anonymous, predatory system.

In Septimus's case, a promising career in an auction house and an ambition to better himself through education has been surrendered to the war effort. Unfortunately, no one seems to respond adequately to his sacrifice. To his employer the war was merely inconvenient because a plaster cast of Ceres got broken and his cook's nerves were ruined. Meanwhile, for Septimus, the war proved devastating. At first he was glad to have emerged from the war without feeling regretful about the death of his friend Evans; but as the months passed he discovered that his vital inner self, his consciousness, was perpetually numbed. Having volunteered to defend what he regards as civilized values – epitomized by Shakespeare and a mental image of Miss Pole, his English teacher 'in a green dress walking in a square' – he now finds that he has lost all feeling for them. Moreover, even his marriage to Rezia in Italy was a sham; he only entered into it because he thought that she would be able to restore his ability to feel through her spontaneity. Their return to England was soured by Septimus's growing revulsion from the external world which meant that he could see no future for society and no point in bringing children into a world which had no meaning. Even Rezia's tears because she has been denied a baby have failed to reach him and unlock his emotions. And, though he recognizes that he needs help, he can do nothing to free himself from his gloom about human nature which has transformed itself into extreme self-loathing.

In contrast Dr Holmes, who comes to attend Septimus at the Smiths' Bloomsbury flat, seems in robust mental health. However, it soon becomes obvious that he is deluded because he fails to recognize the true nature of mental illness, believing that rest and hobbies will act as a cure and consequently patronizing his patients. Septimus is ill because he cannot feel; Holmes is worse because, like the rest of society he cannot see anything is wrong with the world. In Septimus's eyes Holmes represents the ultimate evil ('You brute! You brute!') because he lacks humanity and seeks to deprive Septimus of his individuality. Despite his madness, Septimus recognizes that suicide – death on his own terms – may be the only way to prove his independence from the world and to retain his inner privacy from invasion by others. As he subsides into madness he recognizes that he does at least have a choice: 'But why should he kill himself for their sakes? Food was pleasant; the sun hot.' He remains defiant for the time being.

As the section ends, Septimus has sunk into his own world and is having visions of Evans and of flowers dancing round the room. He recognizes the need to communicate with the outside world, but his mutterings are incomprehensible to Rezia. Holmes arrives at the flat to offer advice and to try and shake Septimus out of his moodiness. Much to Holmes's annoyance, Rezia decides to consult a Harley Street specialist about Septimus.

2.9 **Pp. 84–134**

(a) **Beginning to 'she did not like that man' (p. 91)**

As Big Ben strikes twelve, Clarissa lays down her mending on the bed while the Smiths make their way down Harley Street to Sir

William Bradshaw's consulting rooms. The interview does nothing to reassure Rezia, who feels that a rest-cure will do nothing positive for Septimus because it will cut him off from the one person who cares about him.

The consultation provides Woolf with an opportunity to show another marriage to compare with that of the Dalloways. Sir William, a self-made man, has become so devoted to his career that he has squeezed all individuality out of his wife (in the same way that Peter Walsh thinks that Richard Dalloway has limited Clarissa). His work is gradually providing a 'wall of gold' for the couple, but our attention is drawn to the way in which it isolates them from each other as it grows 'between them'. All the way through the scene he is criticized by Woolf for his lack of humanity: his life is governed by a sense of proportion, and therefore he is unsympathetic to his patients. Above all, he cannot stand a society which permits deviation from what he regards as normal. Sir William particularly dislikes Septimus because he fails to show proper respect for those who are above him in society. Like many other characters in the novel such as Lady Bruton, Hugh Whitbread, Miss Kilman and, to an extent, Richard Dalloway, Sir William tries to impose his views 'on the face of the populace,' not recognizing that this evangelism 'feeds most subtly on the human will' and diminishes an individual's sense of freedom and dignity. In Sir William's case, the theory of proportion and sanity is merely an advanced method of social control. During this scene our sympathy is often directed towards Rezia, and it is obvious that her dislike of Sir William should provide the key towards our attitude, for it is she who has a real sense of priority and proportion which takes account of people's feelings.

(b) From 'Shredding and slicing' (p. 91) to 'So she slept' (p. 100)

Lady Bruton's lunch party for Richard Dalloway and Hugh Whitbread gives us further insight into the way in which the ruling classes in society use other people to serve their own purposes. Lady Bruton, now a powerless old lady, does not particularly like Hugh, but she has invited him because he is talented at writing letters to *The Times*, the most influential British newspaper. Like Sir William Bradshaw, she seeks to bully the lower orders, though with the best of intentions. In her case she is campaigning to persuade the 'superfluous youth of our ever-increasing population' to emigrate to Canada. And although Richard Dalloway makes no objection to the writing of this letter after lunch, we are allowed to see that he does not agree with its sentiments, an insight which redeems him in our eyes because we can see that Woolf is satirizing people who allow a social theory to override their sense of humanity. Hugh is criticized for his patronising attitude towards social inferiors such as Miss Brush, Lady Bruton's secretary, for his superficiality ('He did not go deeply. He brushed surfaces'), and for his insensitive domination of the conversation. Moreover, for all his air of accomplishment, he has had little real influence. When Peter Walsh's name is mentioned Hugh promises to try and do something for him, but we know that this, like the offer to intervene so that Lady Bruton's letter is published, will come to nothing because Hugh has a grossly over-inflated view of his own importance. Hugh is also criticized through Lady Bruton's eyes, for she finds him over-weight and too ponderous when eating his lunch. As with Miss Kilman later, Woolf uses an obsession with eating to indicate her own distaste for the character. Her mockery of Lady Bruton, who is contrasted with Clarissa as a means of showing the reader what Clarissa might become, is made apparent when Lady Bruton falls asleep and begins to snore in a most unladylike way after the gentlemen have left. And yet Clarissa Dalloway and Lady Bruton are united in one respect, for as women they have had to compromise with a world which is dominated by men. The only character who comes well out of the scene is Richard Dalloway, who, reminded of Clarissa by the mention of Peter Walsh, resolves to tell her of his continuing love.

(c) From 'And Richard Dalloway' (p. 100) to 'And he went' (p. 107)

After leaving Lady Bruton's, Richard Dalloway and Hugh Whitbread go shopping. Richard drifts into the expedition because his mind is on other things. The visit to a jeweller's displays Hugh's knowledge about art once again, but it also shows his pomposity because he refuses to deal with anyone except Mr Dubonnet, the senior assistant. We see Hugh through Richard's eyes, though Richard is at the same time thinking about why he never gives Clarissa presents. He leaves the shop determined to take Clarissa flowers as a symbol of his regard for her, for he knows that he cannot bring himself to speak of his love. Despite his inhibitions about expressing his feelings, Richard's concern for his wife and for the unaccompanied children that he sees trying to cross the road as he wanders homewards, show him to be more sensitive than Peter Walsh's view of him would allow. He also shares with his wife an appreciation of the vitality of London and – as he passes Buckingham Palace, home of the Royal family – a sense of historical continuity, despite the horrors of the recently endured war. Above all, like Clarissa, he has the capacity for happiness which Woolf obviously wants to affirm.

Richard arrives home exactly at three o'clock and disturbs Clarissa's thoughts about some of the guests for her party whom she has only invited through a sense of obligation. She is also concerned about Elizabeth's growing regard for the contemptible Miss Kilman. The gift of the flowers confirms the unspoken love between them, despite the triviality of their conversation which is all about the minute doings of the day. As Richard leaves to go and sit on a parliamentary committee, Clarissa reflects upon her continuing relief that they both respect each other's essential privacy, something which Peter Walsh would not have allowed.

(d) From 'How like him' (p. 107) to 'Yet it was a sight that made her want to cry' (p. 113)

Clarissa settles down for her prescribed hour's rest and starts to contrast Richard's capacity for action on someone else's behalf with her own selfish concern about living to savour each moment. She is suddenly overcome with gloom because both Peter and Richard seem to view her as eccentric merely because she puts so much effort into achieving the right combination of people at her parties. She recognizes, however, that the giving of parties allows her an opportunity for self-expression which is otherwise denied. It is her way of defying time and illness. While these thoughts are going through her head, Elizabeth, who is on her way out to tea at the Army and Navy Stores in Victoria Street, comes in to see her; to her annoyance, Miss Kilman remains at the door listening to all that is said. Because of our insight into the workings of Clarissa's mind, we can see that Miss Kilman's resentful view of Clarissa as a worthless parasite upon society is false because it is entirely external. Furthermore, the way that Miss Kilman is described as dowdy and sour is obviously meant to prejudice our attitude towards her. Like many others in the novel, she has a cause – that of evangelistic Christianity – and is condemned within the terms of the novel because of her objectionable streak of self-righteousness: her religiousness is merely a cover for envy. While Miss Kilman waits at the door, Clarissa is aware of a battle going on for dominance over Elizabeth, and when her reminder to Elizabeth about the party goes unheeded, Clarissa feels for a moment that she has lost. However, her laughing farewell deeply offends Miss Kilman, who feels that she is being sneered at and that her possession of Elizabeth is therefore only temporary. Once Miss Kilman and Elizabeth have gone, Clarissa settles down to thinking again, grateful that for all her faults she has never used either love or religion as a means of manipulating people. And it is through this that Woolf seeks to solicit our approval for her. Clarissa watches an old lady who lives opposite climbing the stairs and then looking out of her window, unaware that she is being observed. For Clarissa this old lady is a version of herself – a symbol in her isolation of someone who has been able to retain the 'privacy of the soul' upon which people like Peter Walsh and Miss Kilman try to impinge.

(e) From 'Love Destroyed too' (p. 113) to 'and Elizabeth too' (p. 119)

While she is watching the woman opposite, Clarissa reflects on the nature of love and how it has failed to change Peter Walsh, who is still completely self-absorbed. She feels that those who offer a simple view of life by proposing either love or religion as the solution to its problems are misguided, for neither confronts the central issues of the isolation of the individual and the passing of time, which we are once again reminded of when Big Ben strikes the half hour. Chastened by these thoughts, Clarissa resolves to get on with her preparations for the party.

Meanwhile, we see once again into Miss Kilman's resentment of Clarissa as she walks towards the Army and Navy Stores with Elizabeth. Her religion does little to help her and she feels persecuted by the physical ugliness, accentuated by her poor taste in clothes and her lack of money, which nothing can hide. At this point the reader is invited to sympathize with her – Clarissa's idea of her is not after all, entirely correct. However, her greediness at tea distances her once again. By showing us the scene from Elizabeth's point of view, we are being asked to register an ambiguity towards Miss Kilman. On the one hand she has been badly treated by life; but on the other hand her resentful attitude towards Clarissa's small gifts is unforgivable, particularly as in other circumstances we know that she would surrender herself to pleasure. The contrast here is between two views of life: Miss Kilman's is one of frustrated gluttony because she feels that she is missing out, while Clarissa's attitude is fastidious.

When Elizabeth attempts to leave, Miss Kilman tries to deter her from going to her mother's party, but this merely sets Elizabeth against her because it is transparently inspired by envy. Once Elizabeth has gone, Miss Kilman makes her way past Westminster Cathedral and to Westminster Abbey in the hope that she will gain some consolation for the loss of Elizabeth from God. Some of the other worshippers notice the old and rather scruffy woman at prayer, but they cannot know that her sense of herself as all-important has cut her off from all help, whether human or divine.

(f) From 'And Elizabeth waited in Victoria Street.' (p. 119) to 'Elizabeth Dalloway mounted the Westminster omnibus' (p. 124)

Elizabeth now takes an omnibus from the part of London which is familiar to her – that around Westminster – to the City, the area of London centred on St Paul's Cathedral where the financial rather than the political business of the nation is done. Bothered by Miss Kilman's demands upon her, Elizabeth is conscious of a social pressure on her from other people to be something other than herself. She faces the same dilemma that her mother faced at Bourton many years before. As she rides along she thinks about her future, determining to take up a profession and not to waste herself on trivialities, while at the same time recognizing that her ambition will be thwarted by her laziness. The unfamiliar journey does, however, give her a sense of anonymity and a feeling of liberation from family ties because this is an area of London into which the Dalloways hardly ever go. As with her mother (p. 114), the passing of time forces her out of her dreamy thoughts and back to the reality of her responsibilities. She contrasts herself with the clouds which seem to be free, but the reader knows that they too are subject to uncontrollable forces. She now catches a bus home.

(g) From 'Going and coming' (p. 124) to 'So that was Dr Holmes' (p. 134)

The narrative now turns to the Smiths, who have returned to their flat in Bloomsbury. As Septimus lies resting on the sofa, external sights and noises are exaggerated by his madness and a feeling of joy rises up in him because he feels that nature will help him to defeat the forces, epitomized by Holmes, which threaten his soul. Rezia, meanwhile, sits making a hat, appalled by his complete self-absorption which at times manifests itself in requests that she should write down his rambling thoughts. As she works, Septimus, much to his astonishment and joy, starts to see the world more normally and to take an interest in what she is doing. For a while the visions disappear and the Smiths begin to communicate with each other again through their plans for the hat. A small girl arrives to deliver the evening newspaper. While the Smiths are amusing her, Septimus is suddenly overcome with tiredness and the visions begin again. He finds himself alone and, though part of him recognizes that it is only because Rezia has gone to take the girl home, he is unable to prevent his acute feelings of loneliness which now take the form that Evans is in the room but hiding from him. Rezia's return and her chatter about their first meeting when he was a soldier in Italy helps to restore the earlier mood, but the impending arrival of Sir William Bradshaw's men to take Septimus away creates a dark shadow. Rezia promises that she will not be separated from him, and Septimus is suddenly aware of her as a force which will fight and conquer those who threaten him because they feel that they can judge his life despite the fact that they themselves have an imperfect vision, even though it is one that is socially acceptable.

When Dr Holmes arrives, Rezia attempts to prevent him from seeing Septimus. However, Holmes insists, pushing her aside. It is too late. Septimus, realizing that his wife cannot hope to defeat Holmes, has jumped from the window and mortally wounded himself on the spiked area railings rather than face the offered 'cure'. Even now we are invited to see Dr Holmes's limitations, for as he tries to comfort Rezia he finds it impossible to see why Septimus committed suicide. Moreover, at the end of the section, he advises Mrs Filmer not to allow Rezia to accompany the body, even though Mrs Filmer's instinct is that 'Married people ought to be together.' Rezia falls asleep and dreams of her past with Septimus, which is eventually concentrated into an image of the two of them sitting alone together looking at the sea which, as elsewhere in the book, is symbolic of the eternal rather than the temporal. The last line confirms Rezia's distaste for Holmes's shadowy presence, implying that she has come to a complete and contemptuous understanding of him.

2.10 Pp. 134–46

As he heads back to his hotel room past the British Museum, Peter Walsh hears the ambulance that has come to collect Septimus's body. Once again we are reminded of the numerous different Londons which are created by its inhabitants and those who visit it: they overlap at times, but the connection between them is not often perceived. In this instance, Peter has no idea that the ambulance is taking away the same man that he saw that morning in the park. Peter's introspection reminds him that he is occasionally weak and sentimental and that his failure to make a decent career in India can be entirely blamed on this; however, we sympathize with him because of his appreciation of life's mystery ('life like an unknown garden'), which has meant that he has not become hardened and cynical because of his experiences.

His thoughts move back to his early memories of Clarissa and their youthful theories about how one person can never hope to really know another. Clarissa's idea all those years before was that a person is made up of present and past experiences and therefore can never be known by another because there is an unseen part of everyone. The point is important for our understanding of the novel because Woolf's technique aims to overcome the difficulty of presenting both past and present, inner and outer, when considering her central characters. Despite the infrequency and pain of Peter's meetings with Clarissa since her marriage thirty years before, he is acutely aware of how much his memories of her have influenced his behaviour and how seemingly unrelated external events can suddenly recall a moment of the past to him with extraordinary vividness.

On arriving at his hotel, he continues thinking about Clarissa and the freedom of spirit that she once had. A letter from her breaks in upon the mood because it presents the reality rather than the illusion of Clarissa to him. For all her friendliness in the letter, he cannot help feeling depressed because it reminds him once again of how he lost her and of how her security in life contrasts with his own rootlessness, to which attention is drawn by the description of the characterless hotel room in which he is staying. However, even he recognizes that marriage to Clarissa would have been unsuccessful. As he begins to change for dinner, he thinks about his relationship with Daisy which grew spontaneously and without all the complications of his dealings with Clarissa. All the same, he is bothered by the loss of reputation that Daisy will suffer because of the proposed divorce, and at times he feels it might be better if he merely grew old on his own, leaving Daisy with only the memories of their encounter. He is struck by the way in which he finds women irresistible and yet measures each one in relation to Clarissa, the ideal. For all his insecurity when on his own, others see him as perfectly respectable and composed while he eats his dinner in the hotel dining room. Woolf seeks our qualified approval for him here by noting (and implicitly contrasting him with Miss Kilman and Hugh Whitbread) that he addresses himself 'seriously, not gluttonously, to dinner'.

After dinner Peter falls into conversation with a family from the north of England whom he admires for their solid aims and ambitions in life. During this time he resolves to go to Clarissa's party because he feels the need to break out of his introspection by meeting other people, even if merely to gossip. He sits on the hotel steps alone admiring both the vivacity of the anonymous crowds which swirl around him and the long evening which is unused to because he has not been in England since the introduction of British Summer Time in 1916. As earlier in the day, he rejoices in the way in which England has become more progressive and has overthrown some of the more repressive restrictions on behaviour inherited from the Victorians, symbolized in his memory by Clarissa's Aunt Helena (Miss Parry) who was constantly trying to preserve the past. By now he is walking through Bloomsbury on his way to the party. As he goes he reflects on the nature of happiness gained through his status as an observer of the teeming life which is going on around him. A state of pleasant expectation infuses him until he arrives at the party and realizes that he must behave in a socially acceptable way by presenting to the assembled company the public face of Peter Walsh. As he goes in, a degree of gloom settles over him ('the soul must endure'). This scene, like Elizabeth's bus journey and walk, serves to show the reader the divergence between private and public selves and it emphasizes the city's anonymity as a liberating force, though as we have seen with Septimus Smith, the same conditions can create a morbid mood of isolation in others.

2.11 Pp. 146–65

(a) Beginning to 'here's death, she thought' (p. 162)

Initially, we see the party from the point of view of Clarissa's domestic servants: Lucy, the maid, is excited by the prospect of the Prime Minister being in the house, while Mrs Walker, the cook, is indifferent because she is too worried about whether the food will be well received. Woolf confirms once again through the technique of the novel that all experience is only partial: Mrs Dalloway's party is interpreted in many different ways, and everyone sees a different aspect of it. Only the reader is invited to examine the way in which the various threads of the party are woven together into a whole. Unlikely connections are established between Mrs Barnet, Clarissa's old nurse who is looking after the cloakroom, and Lady Lovejoy, who, though she is at the opposite end of the social spectrum, is drawn to her because they share some of the same past. Later, as Lady Lovejoy is announced at the party, she puts such sentimental thoughts out of her mind, aware that like Peter Walsh she must now present her public self to the gathering. Meanwhile, Clarissa is being watched by Peter as she greets people. She feels that he is criticizing her desire to have parties and that he sees it as a betrayal of her youth. She remains defiant, however, because she feels that this is the one way in which she can make a mark upon the world. While Clarissa is thinking these thoughts she is also involved in a completely different conversation with Lord Lexham and is also thinking about the reaction to him and wondering about whether her party is going to be a success. She contrasts herself with Ellie Henderson, a distant cousin, who is roughly the same age and whom she was reluctant to invite because of her lack of social grace.

Clarissa's thoughts act as a link, and the party is now seen through Ellie's eyes. She rightly feels (and Clarissa does not come well out of this) that she is being patronized because of her lack of money and that she has only been invited to come as a matter of duty. Nonetheless, she decides to enjoy her opportunity to observe a world into which she cannot hope to enter. As with Peter Walsh, both her motive for coming and her attitude are more complex than an outside observer might assume. After she has chatted briefly to Richard Dalloway, the focus of attention moves back to Clarissa, who is starting to feel that her party is going to be a success. She is not enjoying herself, but she does have a sense of achievement. A new group of guests which includes the uninvited Lady Rosseter arrives. Clarissa is astonished to discover that Lady Rosseter and Sally Seton are, in fact, the same person. Once again the issue of each person having many identities arises. Clarissa finds herself suddenly transported back to her love for Sally while at the same time having to maintain her composure as a hostess. Clarissa is aware of how Sally still captivates her even though both of them have changed. She is suddenly called away to greet the Prime Minister, who, as Ellie Henderson thinks to herself, is rather an ordinary looking man. Once again, Woolf is drawing attention to the way in which appearance and reality are often at odds with each other. A further view of the Prime Minister is given by Peter Walsh, who wonders at the British respect for figures of authority, epitomized by Hugh Whitbread who is already pressing forward. Peter's contempt for Hugh is countered by the narrative pointing out that he takes upon himself the role of God by deciding to judge others; moreover, although Hugh is not a likeable figure, he is at least harmless.

The party is seen now as a sea upon which Clarissa (tellingly dressed in 'a silver-green mermaid's dress') floats triumphant; as she escorts the Prime Minister she feels that she is in her natural element, though even now she is conscious of how the passing of time has affected her. Even in her joy she is reminded by the sight of a picture that Miss Kilman hates her. In a way she admires Miss Kilman's hatred because it is more passionate and real than anything in her own life.

As Clarissa mixes with the oddly assorted guests, the reader is aware of how internally past and present mingle. A chance remark by Miss Hilbery transports her back instantly to a memory of her mother in a garden. Clarissa's sympathy is particularly engaged by the young people whom she has invited because they have little to talk about and should be involved in actions rather than words. She also regrets that these people will 'solidify young', whereas in her own eyes she has retained fluidity of personality (though the reader has in fact seen this questioned by a number of other people in the book who see her as stiff).

Our attention is drawn to the artificiality of the party through the conversations of Peter Walsh and Aunt Helena, Clarissa and Lady Bruton. None of these people has anything in common, and they fail to communicate with each other because they are too preoccupied with their own thoughts. Even in small incidents like these we can see that Woolf is illustrating her theme of the isolation of the individual. The superficial success of the party masks its deeper failure to give the participants a reassuring sense of identity and belonging. Clarissa's triumph is undermined both by her own thoughts and also by Lady Bruton's inner contempt for her because she has not really helped Richard Dalloway in his career as a public figure. Lady Bruton is, however, glad to meet Peter Walsh once again because of his recent experience in India. As always, Lady Bruton wants to feel that she is in touch with what is going on in the Empire because being British gives her a sense of identity. She is mocked by the narrative which points out scathingly that she probably assumes that the heaven which she hopes to go to after death cannot in her view be anything other than a British colony efficiently run on British lines.

Just when Sally starts to think about her old friends, Clarissa arrives to reintroduce her to Peter. The narrative moves inside Clarissa for a moment as she recalls how they used to admire Sally's freedom of spirit (recalled through the incident of her unclothed dash down the corridor at Bourton) and assume that she would live her life unfettered by convention. The reality is different because Sally has in fact settled down to exactly the life which she would have formerly condemned. Like the young people that Clarissa was thinking about earlier, Sally has 'solidified'. Clarissa turns away from Peter and Sally to greet the Bradshaws who are very late. Our view of Lady Bradshaw, never favourable, is further coloured by the description of her as a 'sea-lion at the edge of its tank, barking for invitations' because the image shows that she has become little more than a performing animal trained and limited by her husband. The image of her sphere of action as a 'tank' contrasts with both Clarissa and Septimus Smith who are constantly associated with the open sea.

The conversation between Clarissa and the Bradshaws eventually gets round to Septimus Smith. We are surprised to discover that Sir William has at least some humane feelings because he wants to talk to Richard Dalloway about legislation which will help those like Septimus Smith who continue to suffer from shell shock. However, our memory of the way in which he dealt with Smith suggests that his motive is self-promotion rather than altruism. The news about Smith's death suddenly reminds Clarissa that her party is merely a temporary stay against impermanence.

(b) From 'She went on' (p. 162) to 'And she came in from the little room' (p. 165)

Clarissa leaves the main party and goes off into a room on her own, making physical the isolation that she feels mentally, so that she can think about her reaction to the news. At first she feels that the Bradshaws have merely shown bad manners by talking about such an inappropriate subject because it casts a shadow on the party. Further reflection about the details of the death forces her to admire Septimus for his ability to retain integrity ('the thing there was that mattered') whereas she has compromised with life in an attempt to break out of the isolation of the individual. Her admiration is compounded by her knowledge of Sir William (whom she consulted once) and his bullying way of forcing his view of the world onto others. She feels that Septimus is a victim: his life has been made 'intolerable' by Sir William's interference. The contrast between herself and Septimus forces Clarissa to give us a new assessment of her life in which she plainly admits that she has not merely been the innocent victim of circumstance. Instead, she has courted the life which she now has. We do retain sympathy for her, however, because we can see that she had no choice if she was to survive life's harshness. Peter Walsh's solution would have led to disaster, whereas the marriage to Richard, for all its limitations, offers her a refuge.

Clarissa's honesty here raises her in our eyes because she has preserved an ability to be objective about herself. Walking over to the window, she watches the old lady opposite again. The aloofness of the lady and the view of the sky prompts Clarissa to set integrity and loneliness against thoughts of an unsympathetic universe. She resolves to return to her party suddenly aware that if life is to be lived to the full the individual must take account of all these conflicting elements. The striking of Big Ben in the distance (described as 'leaden' to emphasize the point) reminds her that time is passing and that she must face her responsibilities. At the same time, she retains admiration for Septimus who escaped from time's imprisonment.

2.12 **Pp. 165–72**

Peter and Sally sit talking to each other and wondering where Clarissa is. Peter reflects, as Clarissa did earlier, on how Sally has become more conventional since he last saw her on the night that he was turned down by Clarissa thirty years before. At first their only real point of contact is the past. Without being aware of the irony of her own position, Sally outlines how she and Clarissa have drifted apart because she still regards Clarissa's marriage to Richard as a mistake, particularly as it keeps her in contact with Hugh Whitbread who kissed her once in the smoking room at Bourton. Peter agrees with Sally, but at the same moment Sally starts to analyse him, noting that his self-assurance and apparent happiness at not being married is probably a pretence. It also emerges that Clarissa has offended Sally by never coming to visit her in Manchester because she married the son of a miner, even though he is now extremely wealthy. A discomfort that the reader has had throughout the book is now brought finally to the surface, because Sally's view of Clarissa as a snob is so obviously true. What Sally cannot know, however, is that Clarissa is fully aware of her own limitations. And, of course, this is not the whole of Clarissa. A testimony to another side of her character is given by Mrs Hilbery who points out Clarissa's self-abasement. Nonetheless, shortly afterwards Peter and Sally recognize Ellie Henderson and see in her a symbol of Clarissa's contempt towards people who lack both money and status. All the same, they both retain an enormous sense of affection towards Clarissa because she at least always wanted to do the right thing.

While talking about Clarissa's marriage, Sally is suddenly

struck by how little she knows about the relationship between the Dalloways and she admits to herself that her instincts about people are often wrong. Both Sally and Peter watch Elizabeth, contrasting her with Clarissa at the same age. As they do so the Bradshaws leave the party. Woolf reminds us once again of their limitations by showing them peering at the signature on an engraving: Sir William is obsessed with the tidiness of art rather than the chaos of life, and his wife has so much surrendered her individuality that she is only interested in that which interests her husband. Both of them have lost the capacity to feel which Sally and Peter retain and which is, ultimately, what connects them to Clarissa, even though none of them perceive this to be the case. As they watch Richard Dalloway talking warmly to Elizabeth they realize that they have misunderstood him because he does have a heart after all. Sally leaves and Peter suddenly finds himself filled with excited foreboding as he catches sight of Clarissa. And, although the novel ends positively, we are aware of the central theme once again because we know that Peter's view of Clarissa only displays a small part of a much more complex reality.

3 THEMES AND ISSUES

Brief summary of the themes

The above sections will have given you the bare bones of the novel. You should now think about some of the issues which Woolf intends to raise by writing a novel lacking in a central narrative voice which will guide the reader's responses to the characters. Firstly, she wants to show that all experience is subjective: each of the characters perceives life in a different way because each has had different experiences. Secondly, the reader is constantly asked to attend to ideas about human personality being fluid rather than fixed. As we know from our own experience, our behaviour with our friends is not the same as our behaviour with parents, teachers, or those that we are trying to impress in some way.

Woolf takes up this last idea and combines it with an examination of the view that the inner self of each of us is constantly changed by moods or new experiences. What, then, is the true self? Are you most yourself when on your own or with other people? Or is it more complex than that because each of these selves is merely part of the whole? A related point is that our public selves which are on show to others do not truly reflect our private selves which no one ever sees. Woolf is aware that most people are in fact a mass of internal contradictions, some of which may be more apparent to an outsider than to the person himself. In a sense, then, it is impossible to know even yourself fully. Furthermore, Woolf wants her readers to think about the process of getting to know someone else because she recognizes that such knowledge is never anything more than partial.

Mrs Dalloway also shows how people attempt to give their lives a sense of significance and order when there is no belief in God to console them. In Clarissa Dalloway's case, for example, the giving of parties offers her a sense that she is furthering her husband's career and making other people feel that they matter. At its most basic, her life centres on attempts to battle against the passing of time and the inevitability of death. However, people like Miss Kilman (and, to an extent, her old friends Peter Walsh and Sally Seton) view her as the symbol of a society which treasures the superficial and has no connections with the things in life which really matter because it is protected from real emotion by an adequate supply of money. What these people fail to see is that Clarissa Dalloway understands that this protective society offers her sanity because it does not pry too deeply into what she feels. Bearing this last point in mind, we can see that Woolf wants to force the reader to think about how we make choices in life and what the consequence of those choices are. By way of contrast Septimus has no choice because he is the victim of the war and of the economic system. However, his madness does allow him to preserve the central core of his being which, like, Clarissa, he values above all else.

3.1 THE LIFE AND DEATH OF THE SOUL

At the centre of *Mrs Dalloway* is a portrait of her marriage to Richard. To an outsider like Peter Walsh it seems that Clarissa has embraced 'the death of the soul' (p. 53) by exchanging her freedom of spirit and her sexuality for the wealth and security which Richard can offer. His prophecy at Bourton appears to have come true: in his eyes she is 'the perfect hostess' (pp. 9, 56) who has lost all depth and is now merely an empty shell. It is because of this that Peter's question during the morning visit (p. 44) has such urgency. He is desperately attempting to get beneath the social veneer: ' "Tell me," he said, seizing her by the shoulders. "Are you happy, Clarissa? Does Richard –" '. What he cannot know, however, is that Richard, whom Clarissa, Sally and he had mocked initially at Bourton, acts as a source of strength.

When we see Clarissa from the inside we recognize that the veneer hides both insecurity and complexity. Although Clarissa still cares for Peter, she has had to recognize that he trespassed on her inner self too much (p. 9): 'with Peter everything had to be shared; everything gone into. And it was intolerable.' What Clarissa appreciates about her marriage is the way that it offers stability and sanity (p. 164): 'Even now, quite often if Richard had not been there reading *The Times*, so that she could crouch like a bird and gradually revive, send roaring up that immeasurable delight, rubbing stick to stick, one thing with another, she must have perished.' Richard's roses and his solicitousness about her health (pp. 103–7) testify to an affection between the two which allows them to communicate enough to preserve Clarissa's sanity. More importantly, the boundaries between them are clearly defined so that she can retain a sense of self independent of her husband. However, in her lonely reflections on the nature of her marriage (p. 29) she is deeply aware of how much she has missed through her inability to commit herself to him sexually. On the other hand, further involvement would have allowed a rape of the soul.

In choosing to cut herself off from Peter she has surrendered a vital part of herself, as she recognizes when he comes to visit and she suddenly has a sense of enormous well-being (p. 43): 'all in a clap it came over her. If I had married him, this gaiety would have been mine all day!' Deep down she realizes that she has surrendered her desire to feel deeply (we see this when she shies back from the strength of her emotions towards Miss Kilman). Instead mere sensation – an acute awareness of the world immediately around her – has taken the place of anything more substantial. The point is made obvious through the ornate descriptions of everyday life (her view of the florist's shop on page 13 is a case in point). Their extravagance suggests insincerity: Clarissa is trying to create a response to the outside world that she is not sure that she really feels. And it is because of this that she recognizes in moments of honesty with herself that there is something wrong which cannot be cured by doctors or by filling the days with empty sociability (p. 29): 'There was an emptiness about the heart of life; an attic room.' 'The purity, the integrity' (p. 32) of her youthful emotion towards Sally Seton charts how much Clarissa has changed (p. 30): 'Then, for that moment, she had seen the illumination; a match burning in a crocus; an inner meaning almost expressed.' Her desire for privacy has forced her to 'stifle her soul' (p. 68) by cutting herself off from true communication with others. She has made her choice and now, sadly, she has to live with it (p. 43): 'It was all over for her. The sheet was stretched and the bed narrow. She had gone up into the tower alone and left them blackberrying in the sun.'

3.2 IDENTITY AND LONELINESS

During our reading of *Mrs Dalloway* we gradually become aware as we see her from a number of different viewpoints that Clarissa consists of many different and apparently contradictory selves. At times the external picture of Clarissa presents her as being rather calculating and cynical, especially when she is vying with Miss Kilman for dominance over Elizabeth. When she looks in the mirror (pp. 34–5) she sees her outer self as a diamond, precious but hard. At the same time as she is looking at herself as others might see her she is also conscious that the public self does not present the whole (pp. 34–5):

> That was her self when some effort, some call on her to be her self, drew the parts together, she alone knew how different, how incompatible and composed so for the world only into one centre, one diamond, one woman who sat in her drawing-room and made a meeting-point, a radiancy no doubt in some dull lives, a refuge for the lonely to come to, perhaps; she had helped young people, who were grateful to her; had tried to be the same always, never showing a sign of all the other sides of her.

In his long analysis of Clarissa's character Peter Walsh accurately sums up the central paradox (pp. 67–71): 'She had a sense of comedy that was really exquisite, but she needed people, always people, to bring it out, with the inevitable result that she frittered her time away, lunching, dining, giving these incessant parties of hers, talking nonsense, saying things she didn't mean, blunting the edge of her mind, losing her discrimination.'

Even though Clarissa partly depends on others for her sense of identity, she admires the self-sufficiency of the old lady who lives opposite. Like Septimus dying with his 'treasure' (p. 163) intact, the old lady has managed to keep her integrity. Clarissa, on the other hand, has relinquished hers (p. 163): 'A thing there was that mattered; a thing wreathed about with chatter, defaced, obscured in her own life, let drop every day in corruption, lies, chatter.' Her views about the old lady make the theme of the isolation of the individual poignantly explicit (pp. 113–14, 165): 'And the supreme mystery . . . was simply this: here was one room; there another.' For Clarissa, life centres round the problem of being able to balance the need for contact against the need for independence. Her whole life is an attempt to overcome isolation between people, and yet at the same time she recognizes that her successes are illusory (p. 109):

> Here was So-and-so in South Kensington; some one up in Bayswater; and somebody else, say in Mayfair. And she felt quite continuously a sense of their existence; and she felt what a waste; and she felt what a pity; and she felt if only they could be brought together; so she did it. And it was an offering; to combine, to create; but to whom?

Despite such pessimism, Clarissa continues to battle courageously against the forces of time and isolation, though recognizing that they will win. Judging by Clarissa's view of herself (p. 35) as 'a radiancy no doubt in some dull lives', Peter is right to say that (p. 70): 'possibly she said to herself, As we are a doomed race, chained to a sinking ship . . . as the whole thing is a bad joke, let us at any rate, do our part; mitigate the sufferings of our fellow-prisoners . . . decorate the dungeon with flowers and air-cushions; be as decent as we possibly can. Those ruffians, the Gods, shan't have it all their own way.' Thus with her party she attempts to break down the barriers between people, recognizing that some communication is necessary for spiritual health; as Peter Walsh says (pp. 142–3): 'For this is the truth about our soul, he thought . . . suddenly she shoots to the surface and sports on the wind-wrinkled waves; that is, has a positive need to brush, scrape, kindle herself, gossiping.' In Clarissa's eyes the giving of a party gives a momentary sense of significance to life, acting in a way as a substitute for religion (p. 108): 'But suppose Peter said to her, "Yes, yes, but your parties – what's the sense of your parties?" all she could say was (and nobody could be expected to understand): They're an offering; which sounded horribly vague.'

3.3 MADNESS

In many ways, Septimus Smith's story, though seemingly unrelated to Clarissa's, accentuates yet further the theme of the isolation of an individual within society. Once again, Woolf emphasizes the importance of the inner self and the need to retain individuality. The most important similarity lies in Septimus's extreme awareness of his isolation, the 'pit' into which he is conscious that he is descending. The passage in which he reflects that he is 'deserted' (p. 83) exactly parallels Clarissa's panic when she realizes that Richard has gone to lunch with Lady Bruton (p. 43): 'He has left me; I am alone for ever, she thought.' Woolf is drawing attention to his madness as merely a more extreme form of everyone else's sanity.

Unlike Clarissa, he has become oblivious to social pressure; he is no longer able to present an external appearance which is at odds with his inner integrity. Because of his war experiences he is unable to see himself as anything except a brute. Consequently, he refuses to adopt the false identity – that of the decorated war hero – which society attempts to force upon him. He is sympathetically portrayed as a victim of society's definition of normality because society refuses to take any of the blame for his illness. Nonetheless, he longs to connect with other people (p. 84): 'Communication is health; communication is happiness. Communication, he muttered.' However, his efforts to communicate always end with him talking to himself because he now lives in a self-enclosed, dream-world. Whereas for Clarissa there is an overwhelming sense that she must continue trying to make sense of a meaningless world through the giving of parties, for Septimus the world is suffused with meaning, though he can never quite work out what it is. Thus the exhilaration which Clarissa gets from everyday events (contrast their reactions to red roses on pages 83 and 109) becomes for him a form of torture because the natural world takes on a nightmarish and surreal quality and seems to be about to engulf him (p. 22): 'But they beckoned; leaves were alive; trees were alive. And the leaves being connected by millions of fibres with his own body, there on the seat, fanned it up and down. . . . ' In order to preserve his sense of identity Septimus has to cut himself off from the intensity of such a moment (p. 22): 'But he would not go mad. He would shut his eyes; he would see no more.'

Unfortunately for Septimus, death through suicide is eventually his only means of defeating the forces which threaten his inner sense of himself. For him, as Clarissa recognizes (p. 163) 'Death was defiance. Death was an attempt to communicate. . . There was an embrace in death.' And from her point of view, Septimus's true importance lies in the way that he would not allow his soul to be forced by society, symbolized by Sir William Bradshaw and his belief in proportion. He has maintained his independence and his integrity, reasserting control at the last moment.

3.4 *MRS DALLOWAY* AS A SOCIAL SATIRE

The criticism of the upper-middle-class social milieu in the novel is focused by the ambiguous characterization of Clarissa. She is the epitome of 'civilization', and yet at the same time Woolf is mocking the frailty of the values by which her society lives. In particular, there is a degree of bitterness in the novel which centres on the idea that Septimus sacrificed himself willingly during the war in an attempt to defend a society which is indifferent to his fate. Equally important is Woolf's use of Sally, Peter and the past to give us a perspective on Clarissa's betrayal of her youthful idealism and capacity for feeling.

Over the years Clarissa's radicalism has disappeared as has her capacity for passion and love. The point is made explicit by the descriptions of her youth at Bourton which provide us with a way of judging the present. At that time she and Sally (p. 31) 'sat hour after hour, talking in her bedroom at the top of the house, talking about life, how they were to reform the world. They meant to found a society to abolish private property, and actually had a letter written, though not sent out.' In contrast, when Peter visits Clarissa (p. 40) he sees her surrounded by symbols of her complacent acceptance of private property: 'the inlaid table, the mounted paper-knife, the dolphin and the candlesticks, the chair-covers and the old valuable English prints.' And, as we discover later, Peter is uncompromising and unforgiving in his analysis of hypocrisy other than his own (p. 153): 'The All-judging, the All-merciful might excuse. Peter Walsh had no mercy.' We retain our sympathy for Clarissa throughout – but at the same time we see the validity of Peter's point. After all, despite Clarissa's unease about the way that her life has developed, she remains committed (admittedly for reasons of self-preservation) to an existence which Woolf deliberately portrays as superficial and consumed by trivialities. Her 'social instinct' (p. 56) triumphs over her capacity for self-knowledge and analysis. Furthermore, the reader often feels that her philosophy of decency towards others as a means of defeating the powers of destruction and chaos is woefully inadequate, particularly because it is so selective. The issue is well dramatized by Woolf showing Clarissa's snobbish attitude towards both Miss Kilman and her distant cousin Ellie Henderson, who, in Clarissa's eyes, is insignificant because of her lack of money and social grace. Sally Seton confirms this view of Clarissa when she remarks to Peter that Clarissa has never come to visit her in Manchester because she married a miner's son (p. 168). It emerges once again in Clarissa's moment of triumph when she escorts the Prime Minister through her party and feels 'that intoxication of the moment, that dilation of the nerves' (p. 154), particularly as part of the delight stems from Clarissa's feeling that others envy her. What she cannot see is that her triumph is empty because the Prime Minister is so ordinary; 'You might have stood him behind a counter and bought biscuits – poor chap, all rigged up in gold lace.' (p. 152) Even Clarissa feels slightly let down, though she does not quite know why: 'these triumphs (dear old Peter, for example, thinking her so brilliant), had a hollowness; at arm's length they were, not in the heart' (p. 155).

By showing us these external perspectives, Woolf wants to stress the limitations of both her central character and the class which she represents. During her wanderings round London Clarissa shows a sharp awareness of the 'texture' of experience (the early pages of the novel are a good example) and yet her role as a mirror of society succeeds in blinding us with reflections so that initially we cannot see beneath the superficially beguiling and attractive aspects of Clarissa's personality. However, as we read on we realize that at her least sympathetic Clarissa is little better than Hugh Whitbread who, we are told (p. 92) ' . . . did not go deeply.'

He brushed surfaces.' We are also aware that she deliberately avoids thinking about things which she finds distressing. Consequently, she is glad that the grimness of war has ended so that she can view the world complacently once again: 'but it was over; thank Heaven – over. It was June. The King and Queen were at the Palace. And everywhere, though it was still so early, there was a beating, a stirring of galloping ponies, tapping of cricket bats; Lords, Ascot, Ranelagh and all the rest of it; wrapped in the soft mesh of the grey-blue morning air' (p. 6). She wants to see the world through a mist ('soft mesh') so that the sharper edges of reality do not impinge upon her.

The intrusion of Septimus's death into the apparent gaiety adds an incisive edge to the novel's satire. For all Clarissa's snobbish compassion for Lady Bexborough, she has been completely oblivious to the sufferings of those outside her own class as a consequence of the war. Like the rest of her class, she has failed to perceive that she is an unthinking part of the 'civilization' which victimizes people like Septimus. For her the war is over. But the reader is witness to Septimus's continued suffering and cannot help noticing that it is only his death which forces society into a momentary realization of its responsibilities. To be fair, when Sir William smugly suggests to Richard Dalloway (p. 162) that there must be some legal provision for people suffering from the delayed effects of shell shock, Clarissa is the only person who seems capable of feeling sympathy for Septimus as a person rather than a faceless statistic to be viewed with pitying detachment. However, even there Woolf is careful to show us that Clarissa's concern is merely a projection onto Septimus of her own inner worries. As always with the characterization of Clarissa, there is the feeling that despite her good qualities, Woolf intends us to see Clarissa's self-absorption as contemptible self-indulgence.

3.5 LONDON

Throughout *Mrs Dalloway* the reader is constantly reminded of the exact location of the principal characters as they go about their lives in London. Such information is not merely peripheral, acting merely to provide a backdrop for the action. Instead, the portrait of London serves two distinct functions in *Mrs Dalloway* because it allows Woolf to define character through place and it also enables her to dramatize yet further and on a larger scale the central themes of loneliness and alienation which dominate thoughout.

As a native Londoner, Woolf had an instinctive grasp of the way in which different parts of the city could be used to deepen our understanding of character by showing their preoccupations and the world which they attempt to create for themselves. Consequently, the Dalloways' commitment over many generations to 'the tradition of public service' (p. 122) and to the prosperous upper-middle classes is emphasized by their house in Westminster, the political centre of the country. Moreover, when Clarissa goes out shopping she visits only the most prestigious areas such as Piccadilly and Bond Street, thus revealing the geographical and economic limits of the world she has made for herself. The values which the Dalloway family affirm are further displayed when Elizabeth goes on her bus-ride into the City, the financial and commercial centre of the country clustered round St Paul's Cathedral (pp. 119–24): she feels that she is in an alien environment because of its open commitment to trade and financial advancement. In the Dalloway world, money is simply taken for granted. In contrast, the Smiths have lodgings in Bloomsbury, the area in which Woolf herself lived for much of her adult life and which she associated with intellectualism and genteel poverty. It is significant that on his return from India Peter Walsh takes a hotel room in this Bohemian area, for it suggests that he is poorly-off financially and it distances him from the values of the Dalloways, the Whitbreads and the Bradshaws.

The descriptions of urban life also have a thematic significance because they show us how people work to create a niche for themselves so that they can sustain their sense of identity despite the threatening anonymity of the city. The central characters desperately need to prove to themselves that they are part of society rather than merely external observers. In Clarissa's case life becomes an attempt to neutralize such negativity by her commitment to 'society' and to bringing people together. But she is doomed to failure. In part her response to the city centres on 'building it round one' (p. 6) while at the same time ignoring its less desirable aspects. For her the area round Westminster offers happiness and security, and she is unwilling to break out of the known environment even to the extent of visiting her old dressmaker, now retired to Ealing in the suburbs (p. 36). Peter is similarly reassured by familiar sights and gestures such as buying the latest newspaper so that he can keep up with the cricket scores (p. 144). Septimus, on the other hand, is unsuccessful. He is unable to carve out an identity for himself in this environment. His idealism and his desire to make a mark through self-improvement fail to overcome the indifference of the city and his madness estranges him yet further (p. 76):

> London has swallowed up many millions of young men called Smith; thought nothing of fantastic Christian names like Septimus with which their parents have thought to distinguish them. Lodging off the Euston Road, there were experiences, again experiences, such as change a face in two years from a pink innocent oval face to a face lean, contracted, hostile.

Like the lonely wanderer of Eliot's 'Rhapsody on a Windy Night', Septimus remains an outsider. Indeed, our suspicion is that his war experience and madness have merely intensified a situation which existed before the war. It is hardly surprising, therefore, that the first hints of Septimus's breakdown take place when he is surrounded by people and yet seeing them as though from a distance (p. 79):

> He looked at the people outside; happy they seemed, collecting in the middle of the street, shouting, laughing, squabbling over nothing. But he could not taste, he could not feel. In the tea-shop among the tables and the chattering waiters the appalling fear came over him.

The image of the wanderer or the outsider is not, however, always, negative. When Peter Walsh follows the unidentified girl (pp. 48–9) he feels a sudden sense of freedom from the identity given to him by others: 'And just because nobody yet knew he was in London, except Clarissa, and the earth, after the voyage, still seemed an island to him, the strangeness of standing alone, alive, unknown, at half-past eleven in Trafalgar Square overcame him. What is it? Where am I?' (pp. 47–8). Clarissa revels in the same situation when she goes out shopping, because she is suddenly liberated from her responsibilities (p. 11):

> She had the oddest sense of being herself invisible; unseen; unknown; there being no more marrying, no more having of children now, but only this astonishing and rather solemn progress with the rest of them, up Bond Street, this being Mrs Richard Dalloway; not even Clarissa any more; this being Mrs Richard Dalloway.

Clarissa's feeling of freedom is shared by Elizabeth when she leaves Miss Kilman and goes on her bus-ride to the city, thus breaking away temporarily from the roles imposed on her by others (p. 122): 'For no Dalloways came down the Strand daily; she was a pioneer, a stray, venturing, trusting.' However, all three recognize that an escape from their own limited world would cause a loss of identity, and, ultimately, they are glad to return to familiar territory. None of these characters can escape from their background and upbringing and the place in society dictated to them by others; and yet London's bustle offers welcome momentary anonymity and a sense of intense privacy. Ironically, the freedom conferred by the city turns out to be an empty pleasure because it forces the characters into a state of non-being.

Woolf, like many other writers since the late eighteenth century (such as Blake, Wordsworth, Dickens and T. S. Eliot, to name but a few), sees London as both symbol and cause of man's disaffection with his condition. For all these writers London's size serves to illuminate their concern that the complex webs of activity in the city conceal a lack of true connection between people. Like Dickens in *Our Mutual Friend* and *Little Dorrit*, Woolf wants us to be aware of the city as a web of unperceived inter-connection on the part of the participants. The superficial links between the characters (a number of them see a plane overhead; Peter Walsh walks past the Smiths in Regent's Park and then later hears the ambulance that has come to take Septimus's body away) all serve to underline the central paradox of modern city life – the quiet desperation that can be bred from loneliness in a crowd. The point is vividly demonstrated by the fact that even though the people in the novel share the same streets, each of them knows a different London. Indeed, when we think about the connection between Clarissa and Septimus we realize that they live in separate worlds which are linked only by coincidence and the artist's design. Woolf obviously intends that we should sympathize with Sally's attack on the middle classes and Hugh Whitbread for their failure to realize the mutual interdependence which exists between the different levels of society (p. 66): 'she considered him responsible for the state of "those poor girls in Piccadilly" '. And yet the whole of the novel is a testament to how Sally's criticisms can never make any real difference because the structures of society have been bred from inner need.

Consequently, despite the vitality of Woolf's London, it also has a disconcerting and sinister function. It stands in direct contrast to the seeming innocence of youth and the past, as symbolized by Bourton. As with the nightmarish vision of London in Eliot's poem *The Waste Land*, the city displays the distance which exists between people. Paradoxically, despite the infinite possibilities inherent in every moment, city life destroys the opportunities for true communication and closeness between people, replacing them with contact which is invariably superficial. Screens must be erected if a sense of identity is to be maintained in the face of the many pressures put on people by urban life. People cannot afford – as Clarissa recognizes – to give of themselves to everyone, revealing their vulnerability at every turn. But the danger is that the screens which are put up as a defence will ultimately turn into impregnable barriers between people. Perhaps the best concrete illustration of this tension between public and private life is contained in the image of the closed car (pp. 15–17) and the ambulance which carries Septimus away (p. 134). Both are seen as being in their way symptomatic of progress and civilization, and yet we recognize that in Woolf's terms they are modern inventions which symbolise the modern condition, for they allow the occupant to make progress through the crowd while his personality and inner history remains hidden. And it is this dichotomy between public and private which is, after all, central to Woolf's vision.

4 TECHNIQUES

4.1 NARRATIVE METHOD

In her essay 'Mr Bennett and Mrs Brown,' written during the same year (1924) as the bulk of *Mrs Dalloway*, Woolf reviewed the need for a new method for fiction because the work of psychoanalysts such as Sigmund Freud had made people newly aware of the complexities of the human personality. She suggested that 'in or about December, 1910, human character changed'. The date was not arbitrary. It was then that her friend Roger Fry brought the first exhibition of post-Impressionist painting to London and the avant-garde began to understand, through the work of artists like Pablo Picasso, the 'Modernist' perception that people are not fixed entities who can be understood completely by an external observer. Woolf's famous response to the change in artistic climate in her essay 'Modern Fiction' (1919) is worth quoting at length because *Mrs Dalloway* is an artistic exploration of the uneasiness which is being examined here:

> more and more often as time goes by, we suspect a momentary doubt, a spasm of rebellion, as the pages fill themselves up in the customary way. Is life like this? Must novels be like this?
> Look within and life, it seems, is very far from being 'like this'. Examine for a moment an ordinary mind on an ordinary day. The mind receives a myriad impressions – trivial, fantastic, evanescent, or engraved with the sharpness of steel. From all sides they come, an incessant show of innumerable atoms; and as they fall, as they shape themselves into the life of Monday or

Tuesday, the accent falls differently from of old; the moment of importance came not here but there. . . . Life is not a series of gig lamps symmetrically arranged; life is a luminous halo, a semi-transparent envelope surrounding us from the beginning of consciousness to the end. Is it not the task of the novelist to convey this varying, this unknown and uncircumscribed spirit, whatever aberration or complexity it may display, with as little mixture of the alien and external as possible? We are not pleading merely for courage and sincerity; we are suggesting that the proper stuff of fiction is a little other than custom would have us believe it.

Woolf was far from alone in these thoughts about how a new method of writing could reflect the complexity of experience, showing both an internal and an external view of the central characters. She responded warmly, for example, to the opening sections of James Joyce's novel *Ulysses* (1922) which she felt showed that 'Mr Joyce . . . is concerned at all costs to reveal the flickerings of that inmost flame which flashes its messages through the brain.' And, although she became less enthusiastic about the novel, dismissing it eventually as a work of 'genius' which is also a 'misfire,' it is worth remembering that she read the whole of *Ulysses* in August 1922 at exactly the same time that she was formulating her thoughts about *Mrs Dalloway*. Like Proust's massive *A la recherche du temps perdu*, the first volume of which Woolf read in the spring of 1922, *Ulysses* was an inspiration because it showed her that a writer could present the consciousness floating amidst a current of changing impressions without recourse to conventional narrative. Like Joyce, Woolf set aside traditional narrative forms and chose instead to use one day as a fixed, known point for the reader. Using this basic structure she is able to move freely between inner and outer worlds. She can also suggest that there is a difference between external time – the passing of the hours of a day – and the way that time is measured internally. For most of the characters the past is no less alive than the present.

However, there is a major difference between *Ulysses* and *Mrs Dalloway*. Although Woolf is often spoken of as being a 'stream of consciousness' writer, the term must be used carefully because *Mrs Dalloway* avoids the extended internal monologues favoured by

Joyce in which every thought of the character, no matter how incoherent, is presented. Instead, despite her protestations about wanting to show us life 'with as little mixture of the alien and external as possible', Woolf does in fact intervene through her use of what Ann Banfield has called a 'free indirect style'. The internal monologues of a character combine with an external, unidentified voice to give us the impression that there is a narrator talking directly to the reader. For example, if we take the first three sentences of the novel it is obvious that the first of them sees Clarissa from the outside whilst the next two are both external statements which also express Clarissa's thoughts. The method enables us to follow both the characters' conscious, articulated thoughts and also their inner half-realized perceptions about themselves and the world around them. Woolf is not particularly interested in showing us all the absurdities and oddities of human thought patterns. She aims instead for a method which will allow her both fluidity and compression. Consequently, reading *Mrs Dalloway* is a rather odd experience because we feel that we are both inside and outside the characters at the same time. We are tricked into feeling that the author has disappeared, while at the same time Woolf is able to select and manipulate the material which is put before us. The technique is similar to that used in films when the camera seems to rove innocently over a scene picking out incidental details: the scene before us seems entirely artless, but a viewer is being unconsciously influenced by having his attention focused on some things rather than others. Moreover, the fact that the point of view keeps changing (the method has been called 'multipersonal' by a number of critics) constantly forces the reader to see 'reality' through eyes and prejudices other than his own. The clear moral voice of the third person narrator who knows everything and tells us explicitly what to think about the characters (as in, say, Dickens's or George Eliot's novels) seems to be completely absent. Instead, the reader is presented with a number of different views which must be fitted together.

By showing us both an external and an internal view of the central characters, Woolf is able to analyse the isolation of the individual in modern society and the ways in which people mistakenly judge and evaluate each other. This technique helps to create and dramatize many of the novel's themes. Above all, she wants to display the multi-faceted nature of human identity. In her diary for 4 July 1934 she noted of herself: 'How queer to have so many selves,' and it is this which she seeks to convey through her narrative method. Our approval is sought for Clarissa because she shows some awareness of the problem. Unlike most of the other characters, she refuses to judge others by external appearances (though she seems to make an exception in Miss Kilman's case) because she knows how badly she herself has been misjudged by others (p. 9): 'She would not say of any one in the world now that they were this or were that.' Similarly at the end of the novel Sally speculates about the Dalloways (p. 170): 'And were they happy together? . . . for as she admitted, she knew nothing about them, only jumped to conclusions, as one does.' Woolf presents the complexity of the 'real' Clarissa Dalloway by giving a number of subjective views, including that of Clarissa herself. There is, however, no objective view of her. Even at the end she remains something of a mystery, and thus the technique of the novel confirms Sally Seton's thought (p. 170): 'what can one know even of the people one lives with every day?'

Despite the apparent absence of a central, consistent narrative voice certain patterns recur throughout. For example, a number of characters stand on thresholds or view others through a window or a doorway. The motif suggests the conflict between isolation and involvement. Elsewhere, Clarissa, Septimus and Peter all think about their defiance of despair in terms of enjoyment of the 'heat o' the sun', a line from Shakespeare's *Cymbeline*, which becomes a sign of their unwillingness to surrender to the darker side of themselves (pp. 10, 59, 132). Similarly, needlework (such as the mending of Clarissa's dress or Rezia's making of a hat) is seen throughout as being an image of harmony and fulfilment. Consequently, although the traditional narrator seems to have withdrawn, we must never forget that we are nonetheless being directed in our response to both character and situation. Careful attention to these repeated patterns is vital to our understanding of the novel because it is through these that we gradually see the author's preoccupations, rather than those of her characters.

Another major narrative strategy employed is that of the flashback. It has the advantage, as Woolf herself noted when talking about her discovery of the 'tunnelling process', that she can tell the past 'by instalments as I have need of it'. Thus, there is no need to go into lengthy explanations of the former history of the major characters because the past is gradually revealed insofar as it continues to influence the present. It is important, too, from the writer's point of view that revelations about the past come out slowly, because the reader must never forget that the main focus of the novel is the present: 'life; London; this moment of June' (p. 6).

Finally, we are asked to see that the novel's method embodies a truth about how we get to know other people. Despite our status as privileged observers we, like the characters in the novel, are still unable to balance all the different aspects of our knowledge about Clarissa, Peter, and Septimus. Woolf's novel suggests that if art is to capture something of the feeling of real life then life in its full complexity, as we ourselves experience it when dealing with our friends and acquaintances, must be vividly placed before us. And it is this that the narrative technique of *Mrs Dalloway* so brilliantly does. (See also the section on Chronology.)

4.2 METHODS OF CHARACTERIZATION

One of the reasons for the extreme complexity of *Mrs Dalloway* lies in the way that the characters are revealed to us through others. We see what the characters think about each other, but at the same time we have to bear in mind their prejudices: Peter Walsh, for example, is unable to present an impartial view of Clarissa because he is still partly in love with her; Miss Kilman is equally biased because she envies Clarissa her wealth, position, and femininity. Moreover, when the characters are thinking about themselves, they want to see themselves in the best possible light and consequently they may well prove to be unreliable narrators.

However, Woolf does provide us with some external guidelines by showing how people reveal their characters through their mannerisms, their eating habits, their obsessions and their behaviour towards others. Peter Walsh's constant fiddling with his penknife suggests that he is a rather nervous man, as does his restlessness. Miss Kilman's envy of the child who eats the pink cake (p. 116) and her way of 'eating with intensity' is repellent to both the reader and Elizabeth because it shows her selfishness and her inability to give or to think generously of someone else, despite her high-minded Christian principles. Similarly, through his patronizing attitude towards both Lady Bruton's secretary (pp. 92–3) and the assistant in the jeweller's shop (pp. 101–2), Hugh Whitbread displays his intolerance and his insecurity about his own origins. Furthermore, his insistence in pressing flowers on Lady Bruton (pp. 93–4) and his desire to be noticed by the Prime Minister at Clarissa's party (p. 154) show that he is a snob who only behaves well when he feels that he will gain an advantage. His knowledge about antiques characterizes him even further (in the same way that Sir William Bradshaw is also condemned as he looks at the painting in Clarissa's hallway), because it shows that he places value on money and possessions rather than on human relationships.

Secondary characters

One common factor connects almost all of these characters: they unfeelingly force their own wishes on others, though in their own minds they have the best of intentions. Unlike Clarissa they consciously seek to lump people together so that they can undermine individuality and inflict conformity. It is for this reason that Clarissa is set apart from them. She is, as Peter Walsh acknowledges, 'one of the most thorough-going sceptics he had ever met' (p. 70). In particular she loathes the effect that 'love and religion' have on people, because people use them as an excuse for pressing their views on others in order to destroy 'the privacy of the soul' (p. 113). She notices how Peter's love for both herself and Daisy is both selfish and destructive because it is ultimately egocentric (p. 113): 'Think of Peter in love – he came to see her after all these years, and what did he talk about? Himself. Horrible passion!' Sadly, both Peter and Sally, who to an extent represent individualism and the freedom of the spirit, are as guilty as the others because they want Clarissa to conform to their own views. They are seen together with Clarissa at Bourton pouring scorn on Richard Dalloway for his stuffy formality when he announces (p. 56): 'My name is Dalloway.' Moreover, by showing us Peter's love of 'ticketing the moment' (p. 54), Woolf intends us to see that Peter is not truly a free spirit. People cannot survive without achieving a balance between their public and private selves, and it is this imbalance which Sally and Peter would have inflicted on

Clarissa. We are also made aware of how Peter has become rather dried and lonely in middle age. Sentimentality and selfishness have taken the place of vital connection with others. Similarly, for all her apparent free thinking when young, Sally Seton has settled down to a conventional existence in which her house and children seem to satisfy all her needs (pp. 168–9). It is not until near the end of the party that they come to an understanding of how they have misjudged Clarissa's relationship with Richard, and, ironically, the novel demonstrates that Clarissa has in fact retained a freedom of spirit which they have lost.

With characters like Lady Bruton and Miss Kilman, the capacity for doing harm to others is strictly limited. However, both of them try to bend others to their wills in a vain attempt to assert their own importance. The tellingly named Miss Kilman, for example, competes with Clarissa for Elizabeth's affection in order to punish Clarissa for her complacency. Like the other forcers of the soul, Miss Kilman fails to see that Clarissa's outer self is not the whole of her (p. 111):

> Fool! Simpleton! You who have known neither sorrow nor pleasure; who have trifled your life away! And there rose in her an overmastering desire to overcome her; to unmask her. If she could have felled her it would have eased her. But it was not the body; it was the soul and its mockery that she wished to subdue; make feel her mastery.

Dr Holmes and Sir William Bradshaw are much more dangerous because they have society's approval for what they do to others in their desire to impose their own view of sanity on the world. Dr Holmes dismisses all mental illness as mere 'nerve symptoms' and 'funk', and he recommends hobbies as therapy, taking his own life as a perfect example of sanity and balance (p. 82); 'health is largely a matter in our own control . . . for did he not owe his own excellent health . . . to the fact that he could always switch off from his patients onto old furniture?' In Bradshaw's case the public self has taken over his private self completely. He dominates his wife and she is now merely a pathetic extension of himself. At the same time in his professional life he shows the same lack of respect for other people (p. 91): 'He swooped; he devoured. He shut people up.' To Sir William, madness is a form of socially undesirable subversion which must be contained and corrected. Like Septimus, Clarissa recognizes him as capable of 'some indescribable outrage – forcing your soul, that was it' (p. 163). Both men have forgotten how to feel; and, unlike Septimus, they have not felt the loss.

The other minor characters – Richard Dalloway, Elizabeth and Rezia – are more charitably seen. Despite his emotional and intellectual limitations, Richard is well-meaning, both in his political and his private life. His lack of public success is, in a way, a compliment because it shows that he has been ineffective in imposing his will on others. During the course of the novel both his behaviour and all the observations made about him by others serve to convince us that Clarissa did the right thing in marrying him rather than Peter. He is rather dull, admittedly, but Clarissa is confirmed in our eyes as a shrewd judge of character because she perceived that he would provide the stability and reassurance that she constantly needs. Elizabeth is a younger version of Clarissa. Like her mother at Bourton many years before, she is torn between her desire to accept convention and the role assigned to her by others and her desire to make something of her life by casting aside her upbringing. During her bus ride and walk (pp. 119–24) we are aware of her as the timid representative of a new generation of women who are no longer satisfied with their established role in society; it is important to remember that the rights of women were an important issue while Woolf was writing the novel for, despite the Suffragette movement, it was not until 1928 that women gained equal voting rights with men. In contrast, Rezia is, like Clarissa, devoted to helping her husband. She is seen throughout as being both protective and affectionate towards Septimus, even though she is unable to help him during his fits of madness. In particular, she is seen to be a shrewd judge of character during the interview with Sir William Bradshaw (p. 91). Her refusal to be separated from her husband by the well-intentioned but misguided doctors (p. 131) shows her to be courageous in the face of adversity.

4.3 IMAGERY

Although Clarissa Dalloway is only loosely connected to Septimus Smith through the plot of the novel, the link between them is made absolutely explicit through the wave and sea imagery. At the beginning Clarissa leaves home thinking about the morning 'fresh, as if issued to children on a beach' (p. 5) and she takes the 'plunge' into the 'waves of that divine vitality' (p. 8). In contrast, after she has heard of Septimus's death she uses the same word as a means of showing her admiration for his having retained his sense of identity by choosing death: 'But this young man who had killed himself – had he plunged holding this treasure?' (p. 163) Life is seen as being like a sea in which there can be joyful immersion at times such as when Clarissa escorts the Prime Minister (p. 154) through her party like 'a creature floating in its element.' And yet at other times the sea of life is threatening because of its unpredictability (pp. 28–9):

> . . . and felt often as she stood hesitating one moment on the threshold of her drawing-room, an exquisite suspense, such as might stay a diver before plunging while the sea darkens and brightens beneath him, and the waves which threaten to break, but only gently split their surface, roll and conceal and encrust as they just turn over the weeds with pearl.

Unfortunately, some cannot be saved from drowning, as Clarissa recognizes when she contrasts herself with Septimus (p. 164): 'It was her punishment to see sink and disappear here a man, there a woman, in this profound darkness, and she forced to stand here in her evening dress.' Throughout the novel Clarissa feels that it is only the security of her marriage which has kept her from the same fate, and yet as we see with the Bradshaws, marriage may involve one of the partners drowning in the ego of the other (p. 90): 'Fifteen years ago she had gone under. It was nothing you could put your finger on; there had been no scene, no snap; only the slow sinking, waterlogged, of her will into his.'

The sea stands for involvement with other people, a point which is delicately made when Peter Walsh stands watching people setting out for evening parties (p. 145): 'What with these doors being opened, and the descent and the start, it seemed as if the whole of London were embarking in little boats moored to the bank, tossing on the waters.' And it is significant that after Septimus's death Rezia dreams of Septimus and herself (p. 133) 'somewhere near the sea, for there were ships, gulls, butterflies;

they sat on a cliff', because the vision is symptomatic of their being unable to connect with others. However, the longing for the 'caress' of the sea, which offers them both comfort 'hollowing them in its arched shell', suggests that the sea has a dark side and is also linked (as Clarissa knows all too well) with spiritual death. Septimus makes the connection himself in Regent's Park when he is thinking about his inability to feel. His close involvement with war and Evans's death has left him emotionally exhausted and estranged from everything around him (p. 62): 'But he himself remained high on his rock, like a drowned sailor on rock. I leant over the edge of the boat and fell down, he thought. I went under the sea. I have been dead, and yet am now alive, but let me rest still, he begged. . . .' Later on he regards his lack of connection with the world as an advantage because his inner sense of himself has not been corrupted: 'But even Holmes himself could not touch this last relic straying on the edge of the world, this outcast, who gazed back at the inhabited regions, who lay, like a drowned sailor, on the shore of the world.' (p. 83).

The 'ebb and flow of things' (p. 10) which Clarissa so values is often threatening rather than consoling because it draws people away from their true selves. Indeed, as we have already seen, Clarissa's enjoyment of 'ebb and flow' has a great deal to do with her desire to avoid facing the truth about herself. Consequently, the central images of the novel take on much more than a decorative role in the writing because they function as symbolic metaphors which illuminate its themes.

5 SPECIMEN PASSAGE AND COMMENTARY

This section is entirely devoted to a detailed critical examination of pages 36–7 of *Mrs Dalloway*.

5.1 SPECIMEN PASSAGE

Quiet descended on her, calm, content, as her needle, drawing the silk smoothly to its gentle pause, collected the green folds together and attached them, very lightly, to the belt. So on a summer's day waves collect, overbalance, and fall; collect and fall; and the whole world seems to be saying 'that is all', more and more ponderously, until even the heart in the body which lies in the sun on the beach says too, that is all. Fear no more, says the heart. Fear no more, says the heart, committing its burden to some sea, which sighs collectively for all sorrows, and renews, begins, collects, lets fall. And the body alone listens to the passing bee; the wave breaking, the dog barking, far away barking and barking.

'Heavens, the front door-bell!' exclaimed Clarissa, staying her needle. Roused, she listened.

'Mrs Dalloway will see me,' said the elderly man in the hall. 'Oh yes, she will see *me*,' he repeated, putting Lucy aside very benevolently, and running upstairs ever so quickly. 'Yes, yes, yes,' he muttered as he ran upstairs. 'She will see me. After five years in India, Clarissa will see me.'

'Who can – what can – ' asked Mrs Dalloway (thinking it was outrageous to be interrupted at eleven o'clock on the morning of the day she was giving a party), hearing a step on the stairs. She heard a hand upon the door. She made to hide her dress, like a virgin protecting chastity, respecting privacy. Now the brass knob slipped. Now the door opened, and in came – for a single second she could not remember what he was called! so surprised she was to see him, so glad, so shy, so utterly taken aback to have Peter Walsh come to her unexpectedly in the morning! (She had not read his letter.)

5.2 COMMENTARY

Throughout the novel we see that Clarissa is concerned with living each moment of life intensely. During this scene even the mending of a dress takes on a significance beyond itself because it allows her to go in upon herself and to ignore the outside world and the passing of time. As with her party and with Rezia's pleasure in making the hat (pp. 124–8) this is a moment of positive achievement: the act of creation offers her consolation. The pressures of life fall away from her as she surrenders herself to the mechanical process of mending which allows her mind to roam free of her body. Her absorption with the dress gives her a feeling of peace of mind and well-being. Solitariness (as distinct from loneliness) is seen as a means for the inner self to recover from the demands of social contact.

One of the most interesting aspects of the scene is the way that Woolf uses third person narrative to present us with a portrait of her central character. The method also allows Woolf to make her point about solitariness by emphasizing that Clarissa has sunk down into a state in which she has stopped thinking altogether and is merely aware of sensation: the heart (the ability to feel) has taken over from the head (the intellect). This strategy also allows Woolf to present the subsequent moments from both an internal and an external point of view at the same time. We cannot work out, for example, whether it is Woolf who is observing the 'elderly man in the hall' or whether this is Lucy's assessment of him. Slightly later we are given Clarissa's thoughts as though from outside ('thinking it was outrageous') looking in on her, but then for the rest of the last paragraph we see the action entirely from her point of view: 'hearing a step on the stairs. She heard a hand upon the door. She made to hide her dress.'

Clarissa's total concentration on her sewing allows us to see her at her most vulnerable because she is completely without her social façade. It is for this reason that she is so upset to be interrupted; Peter allows her no time to assemble her public personality. Indeed, for a moment she cannot remember his name because she has become so caught up with the hypnotic rhythm of what she has been doing that her public self has almost completely disappeared. Peter's assertiveness in pushing past Lucy flouts the etiquette of the time, and it also dramatizes Clarissa's earlier thought that he lacks respect for the privacy of her soul. Even during his first meeting with Clarissa for five years we see him in his role as a destroyer: he breaks through social conventions and thus threatens Clarissa's marriage, her hard won domestic happiness, and her complacency, by reminding her of what might have been. Repetition of 'She will see me . . . Clarissa will see *me*' emphasizes the strength of the challenge which he presents; and it is not really until he leaves that Clarissa is able to assert her independence from him by reminding him of her party.

The sea imagery and the rhythms of the opening sentences link Clarissa's sewing to nature and to the patterns established elsewhere in the novel. In particular, a connection is later made between this moment and the scene (p. 124) in which Septimus thinks about his former ability to involve himself in life without his sense of identity and individuality being swept away: 'his hand lay there on the back of the sofa, as he had seen his hand lie when he was bathing, floating on top of the waves, while far away on shore he heard dogs barking and barking far away'. For the moment these images seem to arise naturally from the scene before us: the dress is green like the sea (when Clarissa wears it later it is described as a 'silver-green mermaid's dress') and the folds are like waves. In this instance (as with Septimus's death later) the sea consoles the heart by divorcing it from the body and its world weariness. At the same time the waves also symbolize Clarissa's fascination with the minutiae of life. For her nothing should pass by unobserved or unappreciated.

As we read we are caught up by the mood of quietness and calm meditation which has an almost religious quality about it (earlier Clarissa was seen on her own in her bedroom as 'Like a nun withdrawing'). However, when Peter breaks in the intensity of the moment is shattered. Woolf achieves the effect by stressing the order of events in the last paragraph ('Now. . . . Now . . . and in came') thus making the narrative chronological once again. Early on, the writing, particularly because of its wave-like rhythms and its repetitions, seems to take both Clarissa and the reader outside time, but by the end the introspective 'music' of the passage has broken down into discordancy. Peter has forced Clarissa unwillingly back into the 'ebb and flow' of life in all its complexity. Set against the consistency of mood of the first paragraph is Clarissa's confused attitude towards Peter – a mixture of joy and embarrassment – which is to dominate the whole of the subsequent scene.

6 CRITICAL APPRAISALS

For details of contemporary criticism in this section see *Virginia Woolf: The Critical Heritage*, edited by Robin Majumdar and Allen McLaurin.

6.1 CONTEMPORARY CRITICISM

Many of the reviews that appeared shortly after the publication of *Mrs Dalloway* were favourable. One of the most sensitive was by the novelist Richard Hughes in the *Saturday Review of Literature* for 16 May 1925. He admired the novel for its vivid evocation of London and for its ability to make the reader see anew. He also valued Woolf's ability to use form as a way of going beyond the merely poetic and picturesque so that she could show how 'reality' is a subjective construction. More particularly, he praised *Mrs Dalloway* for its honesty in dealing with a central philosophical issue of the twentieth century: that of man's discovery that there is nothing beyond himself which gives order and structure to the world. And, in turn, this perception allowed him to see that the novel has a structural unity which is conveyed through the preoccupations of the central characters.

Here, Mrs Woolf touches all the time the verge of the problem of reality . . . In contrast to the solidity of her visible world there rises throughout the book in a delicate crescendo *fear*. The most notable feature of contemporary thought is the wide recognition by the human mind of its own limitation; i.e., that it is itself not a microcosm (as men used to think) but the macrocosm: that it cannot 'find out' anything about the universe because the terms both of question and answer are terms purely relative to itself: that even the key-words, *being* and *not being*, bear no relation to anything except the mind which formulates them. . . . In short, that logical and associative thinking do not differ in ultimate value – or even perhaps in kind. So, in this book, each of the very different characters – Clarissa Dalloway herself, the slightly more speculative Peter, the Blakeian 'lunatic', Septimus Warren Smith, each with their own more or less formulated hypothesis of the meaning of life – together are an unanswerable illustration of that bottomlessness on which all spiritual values are based.

Woolf herself recorded her friend Lytton Strachey's view because she trusted his judgement and felt that he had hit upon many of her own reservations:

What he says is that there is a discordancy between the ornament (extremely beautiful) and what happens (rather ordinary – or unimportant). This is caused, he thinks, by some discrepancy in Clarissa herself; he thinks she is disagreeable and limited, but that I alternately laugh at her and cover her very remarkably, with myself. So that I think that as a whole, the book does not ring solid; yet, he says, it is a whole; and he says sometimes the writing is of extreme beauty. . . . Perhaps, he said, you have not yet mastered your method. You should take something wilder and more fantastic, a framework that admits of anything, like *Tristram Shandy*. But then I should lose touch with emotions, I said. Yes, he agreed there must be reality for you to start from. Heaven knows how you're to do it. But he thought me at the beginning, not at the end. And he said the *C. R.* [*The Common Reader* – Essays, 1925] was divine, a classic, *Mrs D.* being, I fear, a flawed stone. This is very personal, he said, and old fashioned perhaps; yet I think there is some truth in it, for I remember the night at Rodmell when I decided to give it up, because I found Clarissa in some way tinselly. Then I invented her memories. But I think some distaste for her persisted.

Strachey's doubt about the novel's technique was further developed in 1926 by E. M. Forster (another friend and by now a famous novelist) who felt that Woolf, whatever her other strengths as a novelist, had not yet managed to create interesting and sympathetic characters:

> But what of the subject that she regards as of the highest importance: human beings as a whole and as wholes? She tells us (in her essays) that human beings are the permanent material of fiction, that it is only the method of presenting them which changes and ought to change, that to capture their inner life presents a different problem to each generation of novelists . . . Has she herself succeeded? Do her own characters live?
> I feel that they do live, but not continuously, whereas the characters of Tolstoy (let us say) live continuously . . . And the problem before her – the problem that she has set herself, and that certainly would inaugurate a new literature if solved – is to retain her own wonderful new method and form, and yet allow her readers to inhabit each character with Victorian thoroughness.

Arnold Bennett voiced the same opinion rather more straightforwardly in the *Evening Standard* of 2 December 1926 when he said that 'As regards character drawing, Mrs Woolf (in my opinion) told us ten thousand things about Mrs Dalloway, but did not show us Mrs Dalloway. I got from the novel no coherent picture of Mrs Dalloway. Nor could I see much trace of construction.' In Bennett's view, Woolf's novels suffered because: 'The people in them do not sufficiently live, and hence they cannot claim our sympathy or even our hatred: they leave us indifferent. Logical construction is absent; concentration on the theme (if any) is absent; the interest is dissipated; material is wantonly or clumsily wasted, instead of being employed economically as in the great masterpieces. Problems are neither clearly stated nor clearly solved.'

The most damaging of the reviews in the long-term was that of J. F. Holms in the short-lived periodical *The Calendar of Modern Letters* (1925–7) because he set up the terms by which Woolf was to be dismissed as a writer by Dr F. R. Leavis and his followers writing in the influential magazine *Scrutiny* over the next twenty years. Holms argued that even though *Mrs Dalloway* was Woolf's best book to date, it was simplistic in its approach to human psychology and child-like in its understanding of the world: '*Mrs Dalloway* has the design, apparent intensity, and immediate aspect of a work of art, and it is an interesting problem of aesthetic psychology to explain so self-subsistent a mirage entirely unconnected with reality.' Moreover, he felt that pure description was a poor substitute for 'intelligent novel-writing':

> For this quality of direct sensational perception is precisely that of a child's, undisturbed by thought, feeling and other functions to be acquired in the course of its development as a social organism. And Mrs Woolf is by no means entirely a child; she is thoroughly involved in human relationships, which form moreover her subject matter as a novelist. But her essential reactions to them are a child's automatic reactions, who believes what he reads in a book, who believes life is what he is told it is, that some people are good and others bad – though bad ones are not to be found among persons he knows.

6.2 MORE RECENT CRITICISM

Holms's criticism of *Mrs Dalloway* for being divorced from 'reality' provided the basis for a wholesale dismissal of Woolf's works during the troubled 30s. Many felt that Woolf was out of tune with the times and living in an ivory tower remote from the pressing concerns of her day. Unfortunately, too, Woolf's life became confused with her art. Many people allowed their feelings about the Bloomsbury group as effete and aristocratic to influence their literary judgements. Philip Rahv, for example, writing in 1942, was completely unable to separate Woolf from Mrs Dalloway. In more recent years Woolf's achievement has been more widely recognized. Leon Edel, writing in 1964, praised *Mrs Dalloway* for 'the skill with which Mrs Woolf weaves from one mind into another' and also for the 'prose-poetry' of the novel's style which allows the reader to appreciate the mental processes of the central characters. Edel also points out the virtue of Woolf's method by contrasting it with that of naturalistic writers who see their characters entirely from the outside. He suggests that if this method had been applied to Clarissa she 'would emerge as a commonplace woman, the façade described in detail, but no hint of the fascinating and troubled and mysterious personality behind her exterior'.

Besides recognizing Woolf's triumph with the form of *Mrs Dalloway*, critics have also come to appreciate the importance of her concern with the role of women in society. John Batchelor sees Clarissa as a victim of society's thinking about women because she has been so successfully deprived of any real influence that she becomes unsympathetic towards women who attempt – for whatever reasons – to break out of the role which society has assigned to them:

> In Clarissa Dalloway, particularly, we have the portrayal of a woman who has fitted so snugly into the limitations of being a female that the awareness of these limitations shrinks into the background. It makes itself felt only in forms appropriate to Clarissa's sensibility: the characterization of Miss Kilman, for instance. On reflection one can recognize Miss Kilman as a talented woman who has been victimized by a male-oriented society, but the presentation of her in the novel with her ugliness, her thwarted ambition, and her repressed lesbianism, is designed to affect us as she affects Clarissa; she offends our sense of the aesthetically acceptable.

Nonetheless, within the terms of the novel Clarissa is often viewed sympathetically because she has not adopted the 'warrior attitude' of Lady Bruton who tries to exert influence in the public, the male sphere of life. Instead she is determined to live out her femininity and to let others alone, just as Woolf recommended in *A Room of One's Own*. At the centre of the novel there is a deeply felt concern with the development of women as individuals. For Batchelor, as for many subsequent critics, *Mrs Dalloway* uses the idea of a public and a private life as a means of exploring an opposition between a masculine view of the world (that of doing) and a feminine view (that of feeling).

Various reservations about the novel have, however, remained, and although A. D. Moody's remarks about *Mrs Dalloway* were made many years ago, they do summarize neatly much of what has been elaborated upon since by critics like Jeremy Hawthorn, who suggests that the novel lacks any positive solution to the problem of loneliness and isolation which is at its centre. Moody puts the same case in a different way, suggesting that *Mrs Dalloway* cannot quite decide whether it is supposed to be a social satire or a tragedy and thus falls rather awkwardly between the two. There is finely observed criticism of both the strengths and limitations of a society, but

> in the more ambitious attempt to analyse the vacuity underlying the social facade there are serious imperfections. Without this the novel might have come off as a comedy of manners, a comedy of the *surface* of society, in a mode resembling that of *The Rape of the Lock*, or that of the English cantos of *Don Juan*. It is not less acute nor less amusing in its observations than these; it is only less lively and less consistently amused. And the reason for this is in its attempt to resolve the social comedy into something of a tragedy of the soul . . . .

The crucial flaw in the dramatization of Clarissa Dalloway's 'death of the soul' is that the connexions with her 'doubles,' Bradshaw and Septimus, are not brought home directly enough really to touch on her own complacent image of herself. Moreover, Septimus and Bradshaw are less than convincing in their roles, the latter in particular becoming the mere villain of melodrama. Then again the 'positive' characters who are meant to stand as the representatives of fulfilled vitality, Peter Walsh and Sally Seton, scarcely impinge with any force upon one's consciousness. The net result is that the very grave criticism of a society that kills the soul comes with very little weight or force.

REVISION QUESTIONS

1. '... I adumbrate here a study of insanity and suicide; the world seen by the sane and the insane side by side.' How and why does Woolf link the world of Clarissa Dalloway with that of Septimus Smith?
2. Woolf originally called the novel *The Hours*. Do you think that this would have been an appropriate title?
3. What role does Peter Walsh play in *Mrs Dalloway*?
4. '... for what can one know even of the people one lives with every day?' How far is Sally Seton's remark borne out by the novel?
5. Discuss the importance of the party as the culmination of *Mrs Dalloway*.
6. Many critics have commented on Woolf's ambiguity towards Clarissa Dalloway. Does her ambivalence strengthen or weaken the novel?
7. What part does the theme of marriage play in *Mrs Dalloway*?
8. Show how Woolf uses the technique of *Mrs Dalloway* to create some of its themes.
9. Is *Mrs Dalloway* anything more than a simple social comedy told in an unnecessarily complex way?
10. Would you agree with the opinion that *Mrs Dalloway* is a bitter condemnation of the priorities of a society which has lost all sense of value and direction?
11. What does *Mrs Dalloway* suggest about Woolf's views about how women were treated by society in the 1920s?
12. How successful is Woolf in creating the atmosphere of London during the years after the First World War?

FURTHER READING

Other books by Virginia Woolf which may shed light on *Mrs Dalloway* are:
The Voyage Out (Duckworth, 1915).
Mr Bennett and Mrs Brown (Hogarth, 1924) – Critical Essays.
The Common Reader (Hogarth, 1925) – Critical Essays.
To the Lighthouse (Hogarth, 1927).
A Room of One's Own (Hogarth, 1928).
The Common Reader: Second Series (Hogarth, 1932).
A Writer's Diary: Extracts from the Diary of Virginia Woolf, edited by Leonard Woolf (Hogarth, 1953).

Biography

The standard biography is that by Quentin Bell, *Virginia Woolf: A Biography*, 2 vols (Hogarth, 1972). There is also a critical biography by Lyndall Gordon, *Virginia Woolf: A Writer's Life* (Oxford, 1984).

Topography

There is an extensive description of the background to the novel in the chapter 'Virginia Woolf's London' in *Literary Landscapes of the British Isles* by David Daiches and John Flower (Penguin, 1981).

Criticism

Fleishman, Avrom, *Virginia Woolf: A Critical Reading* (Johns Hopkins, 1975).
Hawthorn, Jeremy, *Virginia Woolf's Mrs Dalloway: A Study in Alienation* (Sussex University Press, 1975).
Majumdar, Robin and Allen Mc Laurin (eds) *Virginia Woolf: The Critical Heritage* (Routledge and Kegan Paul, 1975).
Moody, A. D., *Virginia Woolf* (Oliver and Boyd, 1963).
Sprague, Claire (ed.), *Virginia Woolf: A Collection of Critical Essays* (Prentice-Hall, 1971).

Mastering English Literature
Richard Gill

Mastering English Literature will help readers both to enjoy English Literature and to be successful in 'O' levels, 'A' levels and other public exams. It is an introduction to the study of poetry, novels and drama which helps the reader in four ways - by providing ways of approaching literature, by giving examples and practice exercises, by offering hints on how to write about literature, and by the author's own evident enthusiasm for the subject. With extracts from more than 200 texts, this is an enjoyable account of how to get the maximum satisfaction out of reading, whether it be for formal examinations or simply for pleasure.

Work Out English Literature ('A' level)
S.H. Burton

This book familiarises 'A' level English Literature candidates with every kind of test which they are likely to encounter. Suggested answers are worked out step by step and accompanied by full author's commentary. The book helps students to clarify their aims and establish techniques and standards so that they can make appropriate responses to similar questions when the examination pressures are on. It opens up fresh ways of looking at the full range of set texts, authors and critical judgements and motivates students to know more of these matters.

MACMILLAN STUDENTS' NOVELS

General Editor: JAMES GIBSON

The Macmillan Students' Novels are low-priced, new editions of major classics, aimed at the first examination candidate. Each volume contains:

* enough explanation and background material to make the novels accessible — and rewarding — to pupils with little or no previous knowledge of the author or the literary period;

* detailed notes elucidate matters of vocabulary, interpretation and historical background;

* eight pages of plates comprising facsimiles of manuscripts and early editions, portraits of the author and photographs of the geographical setting of the novels.

JANE AUSTEN: MANSFIELD PARK
Editor: Richard Wirdnam

JANE AUSTEN: NORTHANGER ABBEY
Editor: Raymond Wilson

JANE AUSTEN: PRIDE AND PREJUDICE
Editor: Raymond Wilson

JANE AUSTEN: SENSE AND SENSIBILITY
Editor: Raymond Wilson

JANE AUSTEN: PERSUASION
Editor: Richard Wirdnam

CHARLOTTE BRONTË: JANE EYRE
Editor: F. B. Pinion

EMILY BRONTË: WUTHERING HEIGHTS
Editor: Graham Handley

JOSEPH CONRAD: LORD JIM
Editor: Peter Hollindale

CHARLES DICKENS: GREAT EXPECTATIONS
Editor: James Gibson

CHARLES DICKENS: HARD TIMES
Editor: James Gibson

CHARLES DICKENS: OLIVER TWIST
Editor: Guy Williams

CHARLES DICKENS: A TALE OF TWO CITIES
Editor: James Gibson

GEORGE ELIOT: SILAS MARNER
Editor: Norman Howlings

GEORGE ELIOT: THE MILL ON THE FLOSS
Editor: Graham Handley

D. H. LAWRENCE: SONS AND LOVERS
Editor: James Gibson

D. H. LAWRENCE: THE RAINBOW
Editor: James Gibson

MARK TWAIN: HUCKLEBERRY FINN
Editor: Christopher Parry

Also from Macmillan

CASEBOOK SERIES

The Macmillan *Casebook* series brings together the best of modern criticism with a selection of early reviews and comments. Each Casebook charts the development of opinion on a play, poem, or novel, or on a literary genre, from its first appearance to the present day.

GENERAL THEMES

COMEDY: DEVELOPMENTS IN CRITICISM
D. J. Palmer

DRAMA CRITICISM: DEVELOPMENTS SINCE IBSEN
A. J. Hinchliffe

THE ENGLISH NOVEL: DEVELOPMENTS IN CRITICISM SINCE HENRY JAMES
Stephen Hazell

THE LANGUAGE OF LITERATURE
N. Page

THE PASTORAL MODE
Bryan Loughrey

THE ROMANTIC IMAGINATION
J. S. Hill

TRAGEDY: DEVELOPMENTS IN CRITICISM
R. P. Draper

POETRY

WILLIAM BLAKE: SONGS OF INNOCENCE AND EXPERIENCE
Margaret Bottrall

BROWNING: MEN AND WOMEN AND OTHER POEMS
J. R. Watson

BYRON: CHILDE HAROLD'S PILGRIMAGE AND DON JUAN
John Jump

CHAUCER: THE CANTERBURY TALES
J. J. Anderson

COLERIDGE: THE ANCIENT MARINER AND OTHER POEMS
A. R. Jones and W. Tydeman

DONNE: SONGS AND SONETS
Julian Lovelock

T. S. ELIOT: FOUR QUARTETS
Bernard Bergonzi

T. S. ELIOT: PRUFROCK, GERONTION, ASH WEDNESDAY AND OTHER POEMS
B. C. Southam

T. S. ELIOT: THE WASTELAND
C. B. Cox and A. J. Hinchliffe

ELIZABETHAN POETRY: LYRICAL AND NARRATIVE
Gerald Hammond

THOMAS HARDY: POEMS
J. Gibson and T. Johnson

GERALD MANLEY HOPKINS: POEMS
Margaret Bottrall

KEATS: ODES
G. S. Fraser

KEATS: THE NARRATIVE POEMS
J. S. Hill

MARVELL: POEMS
Arthur Pollard

THE METAPHYSICAL POETS
Gerald Hammond

MILTON: PARADISE LOST
A. E. Dyson and Julian Lovelock

POETRY OF THE FIRST WORLD WAR
Dominic Hibberd

ALEXANDER POPE: THE RAPE OF THE LOCK
John Dixon Hunt

SHELLEY: SHORTER POEMS & LYRICS
Patrick Swinden

SPENSER: THE FAERIE QUEEN
Peter Bayley

TENNYSON: IN MEMORIAM
John Dixon Hunt

THIRTIES POETS: 'THE AUDEN GROUP'
Ronald Carter

WORDSWORTH: LYRICAL BALLADS
A. R. Jones and W. Tydeman

WORDSWORTH: THE PRELUDE
W. J. Harvey and R. Gravil

W. B. YEATS: POEMS 1919-1935
E. Cullingford

W. B. YEATS: LAST POEMS
Jon Stallworthy

THE NOVEL AND PROSE

JANE AUSTEN: EMMA
David Lodge

JANE AUSTEN: NORTHANGER ABBEY AND PERSUASION
B. C. Southam

JANE AUSTEN: SENSE AND SENSIBILITY, PRIDE AND PREJUDICE AND MANSFIELD PARK
B. C. Southam

CHARLOTTE BRONTË: JANE EYRE AND VILLETTE
Miriam Allott

EMILY BRONTË: WUTHERING HEIGHTS
Miriam Allott

BUNYAN: THE PILGRIM'S PROGRESS
R. Sharrock

CONRAD: HEART OF DARKNESS, NOSTROMO AND UNDER WESTERN EYES
C. B. Cox

CONRAD: THE SECRET AGENT
Ian Watt

CHARLES DICKENS: BLEAK HOUSE
A. E. Dyson

CHARLES DICKENS: DOMBEY AND SON AND LITTLE DORRITT
Alan Shelston

CHARLES DICKENS: HARD TIMES, GREAT EXPECTATIONS AND OUR MUTUAL FRIEND
N. Page

GEORGE ELIOT: MIDDLEMARCH
Patrick Swinden

GEORGE ELIOT: THE MILL ON THE FLOSS AND SILAS MARNER
R. P. Draper

HENRY FIELDING: TOM JONES
Neil Compton

E. M. FORSTER: A PASSAGE TO INDIA
Malcolm Bradbury

HARDY: THE TRAGIC NOVELS
R. P. Draper

HENRY JAMES: WASHINGTON SQUARE AND THE PORTRAIT OF A LADY
Alan Shelston

JAMES JOYCE: DUBLINERS AND A PORTRAIT OF THE ARTIST AS A YOUNG MAN
Morris Beja

D. H. LAWRENCE: THE RAINBOW AND WOMEN IN LOVE
Colin Clarke

D. H. LAWRENCE: SONS AND LOVERS
Gamini Salgado

SWIFT: GULLIVER'S TRAVELS
Richard Gravil

THACKERAY: VANITY FAIR
Arthur Pollard

TROLLOPE: THE BARSETSHIRE
NOVELS
T. Bareham

VIRGINIA WOOLF: TO THE
LIGHTHOUSE
Morris Beja

DRAMA

CONGREVE: COMEDIES
Patrick Lyons

T. S. ELIOT: PLAYS
Arnold P. Hinchliffe

JONSON: EVERY MAN IN HIS
HUMOUR AND THE ALCHEMIST
R. V. Holdsworth

JONSON: VOLPONE
J. A. Barish

MARLOWE: DR FAUSTUS
John Jump

MARLOWE: TAMBURLAINE,
EDWARD II AND THE JEW OF
MALTA
John Russell Brown

MEDIEVAL ENGLISH DRAMA
Peter Happé

O'CASEY: JUNO AND THE
PAYCOCK, THE PLOUGH AND THE
STARS AND THE SHADOW OF A
GUNMAN
R. Ayling

JOHN OSBORNE: LOOK BACK IN
ANGER
John Russell Taylor

WEBSTER: THE WHITE DEVIL AND
THE DUCHESS OF MALFI
R. V. Holdsworth

WILDE: COMEDIES
W. Tydeman

SHAKESPEARE

SHAKESPEARE: ANTONY AND
CLEOPATRA
John Russell Brown

SHAKESPEARE: CORIOLANUS
B. A. Brockman

SHAKESPEARE: HAMLET
John Jump

SHAKESPEARE: HENRY IV PARTS
I AND II
G. K. Hunter

SHAKESPEARE: HENRY V
Michael Quinn

SHAKESPEARE: JULIUS CAESAR
Peter Ure

SHAKESPEARE: KING LEAR
Frank Kermode

SHAKESPEARE: MACBETH
John Wain

SHAKESPEARE: MEASURE FOR
MEASURE
G. K. Stead

SHAKESPEARE: THE MERCHANT
OF VENICE
John Wilders

SHAKESPEARE: A MIDSUMMER
NIGHT'S DREAM
A. W. Price

SHAKESPEARE: MUCH ADO
ABOUT NOTHING AND AS YOU
LIKE IT
John Russell Brown

SHAKESPEARE: OTHELLO
John Wain

SHAKESPEARE: RICHARD II
N. Brooke

SHAKESPEARE: THE SONNETS
Peter Jones

SHAKESPEARE: THE TEMPEST
D. J. Palmer

SHAKESPEARE: TROILUS AND
CRESSIDA
Priscilla Martin

SHAKESPEARE: TWELFTH NIGHT
D. J. Palmer

SHAKESPEARE: THE WINTER'S
TALE
Kenneth Muir

THE MACMILLAN SHAKESPEARE

General Editor: PETER HOLLINDALE
Advisory Editor: PHILIP BROCKBANK

The Macmillan Shakespeare features:
* clear and uncluttered texts with modernised punctuation and spelling wherever possible;
* full explanatory notes printed on the page facing the relevant text for ease of reference;
* stimulating introductions which concentrate on content, dramatic effect, character and imagery, rather than mere dates and sources.

Above all, The Macmillan Shakespeare treats each play as a work for the theatre which can also be enjoyed on the page.

CORIOLANUS
Editor: Tony Parr

THE WINTER'S TALE
Editor: Christopher Parry

MUCH ADO ABOUT NOTHING
Editor: Jan McKeith

RICHARD II
Editor: Richard Adams

RICHARD III
Editor: Richard Adams

HENRY IV, PART I
Editor: Peter Hollindale

HENRY IV, PART II
Editor: Tony Parr

HENRY V
Editor: Brian Phythian

AS YOU LIKE IT
Editor: Peter Hollindale

A MIDSUMMER NIGHT'S DREAM
Editor: Norman Sanders

THE MERCHANT OF VENICE
Editor: Christopher Parry

THE TAMING OF THE SHREW
Editor: Robin Hood

TWELFTH NIGHT
Editor: E. A. J. Honigmann

THE TEMPEST
Editor: A. C. Spearing

ROMEO AND JULIET
Editor: James Gibson

JULIUS CAESAR
Editor: D. R. Elloway

MACBETH
Editor: D. R. Elloway

HAMLET
Editor: Nigel Alexander

ANTONY AND CLEOPATRA
Editors: Jan McKeith and Richard Adams

OTHELLO
Editors: Celia Hilton and R. T. Jones

KING LEAR
Editor: Philip Edwards

MACMILLAN SHAKESPEARE VIDEO WORKSHOPS

DAVID WHITWORTH

Three unique book and video packages, each examining a particular aspect of Shakespeare's work; tragedy, comedy and the Roman plays. Designed for all students of Shakespeare, each package assumes no previous knowledge of the plays and can serve as a useful introduction to Shakespeare for 'O' and 'A' level candidates as well as for students at colleges and institutes of further, higher and adult education.

The material is based on the New Shakespeare Company Workshops at the Roundhouse, adapted and extended for television. By combining the resources of television and a small theatre company, this exploration of Shakespeare's plays offers insights into varied interpretations, presentation, styles of acting as well as useful background information.

While being no substitute for seeing the whole plays in performance, it is envisaged that these video cassettes will impart something of the original excitement of the theatrical experience, and serve as a welcome complement to textual analysis leading to an enriched and broader view of the plays.

Each package consists of:

* the Macmillan Shakespeare editions of the plays concerned;
* a video cassette available in VHS or Beta;
* a leaflet of teacher's notes.

THE TORTURED MIND
looks at the four tragedies Hamlet, Othello, Macbeth and King Lear.

THE COMIC SPIRIT
examines the comedies Much Ado About Nothing, Twelfth Night, A Midsummer Night's Dream, and As You Like It.

THE ROMAN PLAYS
Features Julius Caesar, Antony and Cleopatra and Coriolanus